A-Z W____

C000183361

CON____

REFERENCE

Motorway	M53	Car Park (selected)	P
A Road	A551	Church or Chapel	†
Tunnel		Cycleway (selected)	☞
B Road	B5138	Fire Station	■
Dual Carriageway		Hospital	H
One-way Street	→	House Numbers (A & B Roads only)	13 8
Traffic flow on A Roads is indicated by a heavy line on the driver's left.		Information Centre	i
		National Grid Reference	340
Restricted Access		Police Station	▲
Pedestrianized Road		Post Office	★
Track / Footpath		Toilet:	
		without facilities for the Disabled	▽
		with facilities for the Disabled	▽
Railway	Station / Level Crossing / Tunnel	Disabled facilities only	▽
		Viewpoint	米 ☀
Built-up Area	GLAMIS Cl.	Educational Establishment	◰
		Hospital or Hospice	◰
Local Authority Boundary	— ·· — ·· —	Industrial Building	◰
Posttown Boundary		Leisure or Recreational Facility	◰
Postcode Boundary within Posttown	— — —	Place of Interest	◰
		Public Building	◰
		Shopping Centre or Market	◰
Map Continuation	▲ 20	Other Selected Buildings	◰

SCALE

1:15,840   4 inches to 1 mile   **SCALE**   6.31 cm to 1 km   10.16 cm to 1 mile

0   ¼   ½   ¾   1 Mile

0   250   500   750   1 Kilometre

Copyright of Geographers' A-Z Map Company Limited

Fairfield Road, Borough Green, Sevenoaks, Kent TN15 8PP
Telephone: 01732 781000 (Enquiries & Trade Sales)
01732 783422 (Retail Sales)

www.a-zmaps.co.uk

Copyright © Geographers' A-Z Map Co. Ltd.

Ordnance Survey® This product includes mapping data licensed from Ordnance Survey® with the permission of the Controller of Her Majesty's Stationery Office.

© Crown Copyright 2004. All rights reserved. Licence number 100017302

Edition 4* 2005

KEY TO MAP PAGES

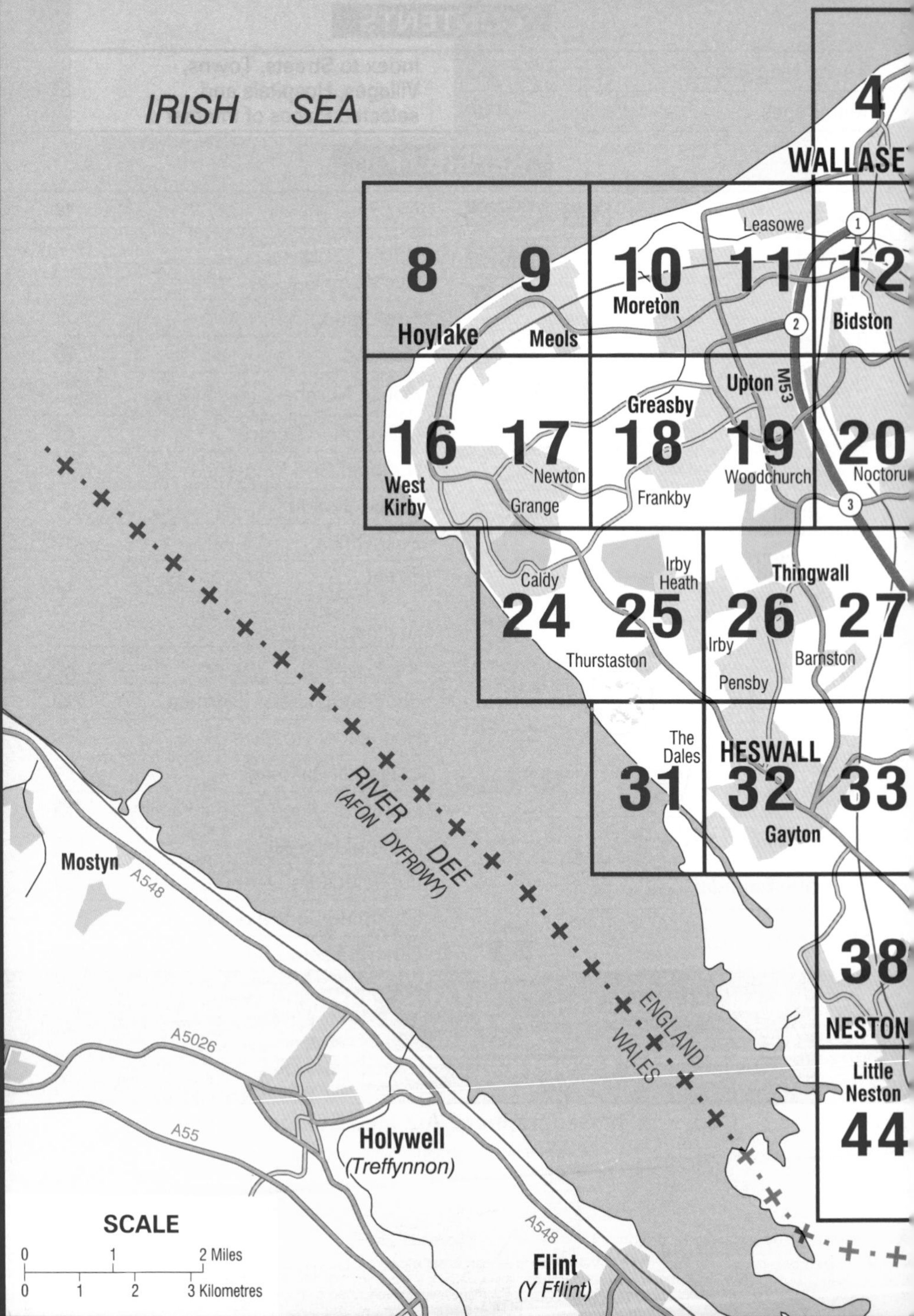

IRISH SEA

4

WALLASE

Leasowe ①

8 **9** **10** **11** **12**

Moreton

Hoylake **Meols** ② **Bidston**

Upton

M53

Greasby

16 **17** **18** **19** **20**

West
Kirby Newton Frankby Woodchurch Noctoru

Grange ③

Thingwall

Irby
Heath

Caldy **24** **25** **26** **27**

Irby

Thurstaston Pensby Barnston

The
Dales **HESWALL**

31 **32** **33**

Gayton

Mostyn A548

38

A5026

NESTON

Little
Neston

A55

ENGLAND
WALES

44

RIVER DEE
(AFON DYFRDWY)

Holywell
(Treffynnon)

SCALE

0 1 2 Miles

0 1 2 3 Kilometres

A548

Flint
(Y Fflint)

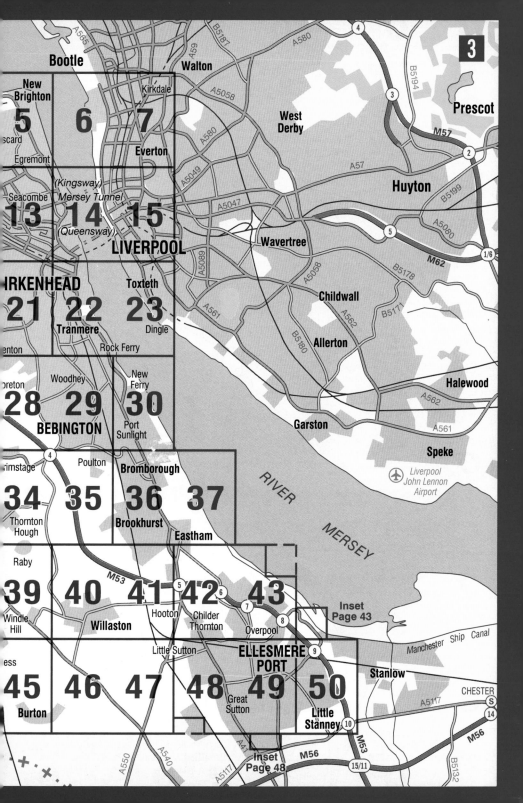

A · B · C · D

6 1 2 3 4 5 6

94

93

92

BOOTLE

MILLERS

L3

RIVER MERSEY

SEFTON
LIVERPOOL
WIRRAL

5

Egremont

Alexandra Dock

Branch Dock (No2)

Branch Dock (No. 1)

Langton Dock

Brocklebank Dock

Branch Dock

Canada Branch Dock (No. 3)

Canada Dock

Canada Branch Dock (No. 2)

Canada Graving Dock

Canada Branch Dock (No. 1)

Huskisson Branch Dock (No.3)

Huskisson Dock

Huskisson Branch Dock (No.1)

Sandon Dock Wastewater Treatment Works

Sandon Half Tide Dock

Wellington Dock

Bramley Moore Dock

Nelson Dock

Swing-bridge

Collingwood Dock
Bascule Bri.

Victoria Tower

Salisbury Dock

Bascule Bridge

Stanley Dock

Stanley Warehouses

Warehouse

BANKFIELD

BELLTOWER

SANDH

SANDON INDUSTRIAL ESTATE

DERBY

BOUNDARY ST.

Atlantic Park

STREET

BLACKSTONE ST.

Super-store

ATHOL AVE

HOWARD

Vaux

CHURCH ST.

REGENT ROAD

Depot

Works

Depot

GRIMSHAW ST.

DERBY

A5036

A5058

A5065

NELSON

SEYMOUR

EFFINGHAM ST.

NAPIER ST.

HOWE ST.

KEPPEL ST.

DRAKE ST.

DUNDAS ST.

BERESFORD ST.

RALEIGH ST.

DACRE

WILLIAM

HENRY

PRINCES

BEDFORD

ENSOR'S

BRUNSWICK PL

DWR. BANK VIEW

Dep

GRUNC

WALTER ST.

SALTNEY ST.

DUBLIN ST.

DICKSON ST.

COTTON

GREAT

PROMENADE

STRE

A   **B**   21   **C**   **D**

1

IRISH   SEA

2

EAST

91

3

LIVERPOOL

4

390

5

Model
Boating Pond

HOYLAKE   Comm.
Cen.

Jetty

Lifeboat
Station

SANDPIPERS
CT.

P A R A D E

CLYDE DOVEDALE
AVONDALE
RD.
FERNDALE

T R I N
STRAND RD.
LAKE RD.
MARMION
SEA VIEW
GOVERNMENT RD.
ALDERLEY

Rec.
Grd.

GROVE RD.
LAKE
GROVE

SHAW RD.
CUMBERLAND RD.
EVANS VALLEY RD.

6

N O R T H

LABLE

MARINE
QUEEN'S RD.
WARREN RD.

THE KINGS
CURZON RD.
CROWN RD.

CHERRY
GDS.

ROAD
KINGS

M A R K E T
A553

89

A   **B**   **16**   **C**   **D**

COURTENAY RD.
MARCH
STREET
BARTON
21
ROSECROFT
CT.

STANLEY ROAD
VALENTIA RD.
LIGHTHOUSE RD.
GAP
MONTROSE
GROSVENOR RD.

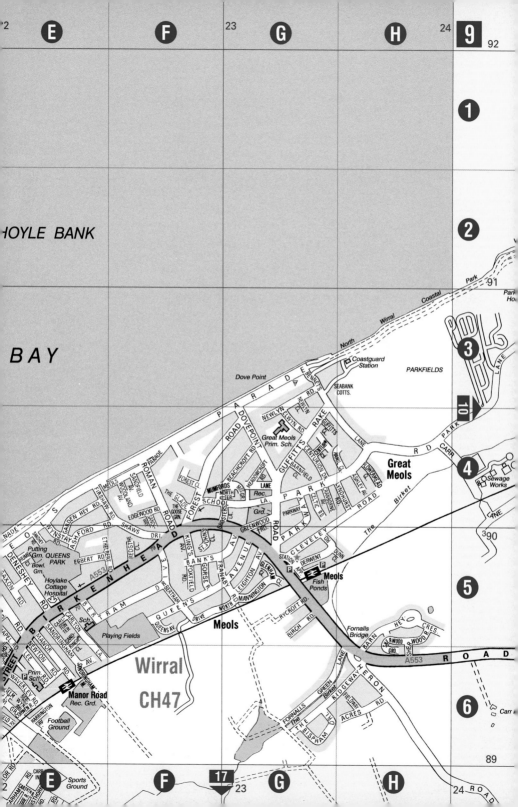

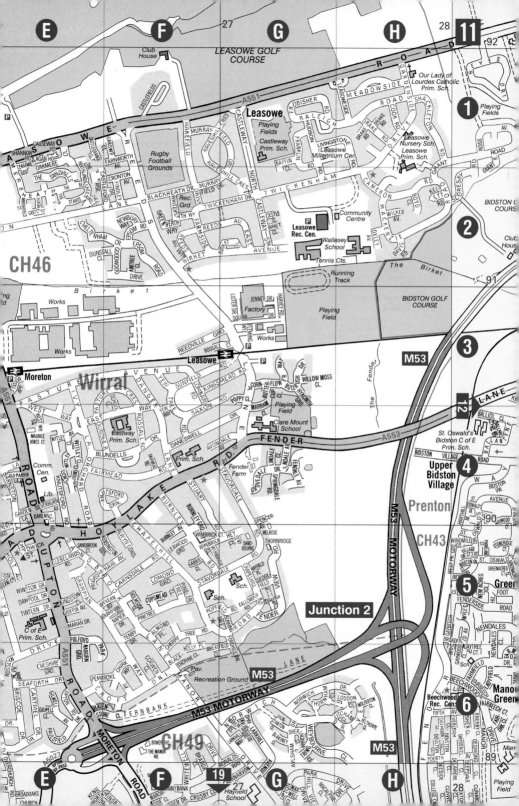

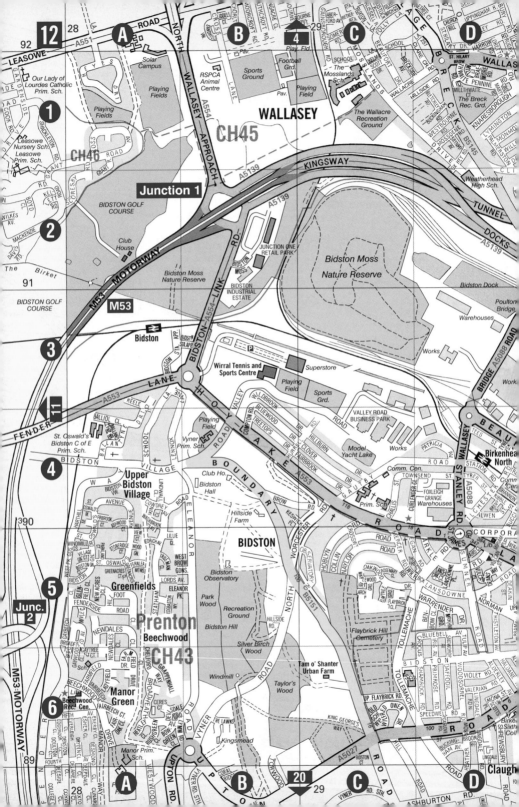

RIVER MERSEY

KINGSWAY (MERSEY TUNNEL - TOLL)

LIVERPOOL

Birkenhead CH41

QUEENSWAY (MERSEY TUNNEL - TOLL)

LIVERPOOL WIRRAL

BIRKENHEAD

Guinea Gap Baths and Rec. Cen.

Seacombe Ship Ferry (Foot) Terminal

Floating Stage

Bus Station

Factory

Seacombe

Alfred Pier Head

Dock Masters Office

Alfred Lock

Alfred Dock

Bascule Bridge

MORTAR MILL QUAY

Twelve Quays Ferry Terminal

EAST FLOAT

390

DOCKS

Tower Quays

Egerton Dock

Morpeth Dock

Morpeth Wharf

Sewage Works

Birkenhead Transport Mus.

Wirral Transport Mus.

Woodside Bus Park

Hamilton Sq. Gall.

Great LWestern House

Rosebrae Ct.

Conway Pk.

Europa Pools

Vue Cin.

Waterloo Lock

Waterloo River Entrance

West Waterloo Dock

East Waterloo Dock

Princes Half Tide Dock

Princes Jetty

Princes Dock

Offices

Liverpool Landing Stage

Ship Ferry (Foot) Terminal

Pier Head

Museum of Liverpool Life

Tate Gallery

Trafalgar Dock

Ferry Terminal

Depot

Collingwood Dock

Salisbury Dock

Salisbury Dock Bascule Bri.

Victoria Tower

Stanley Dock

Superstore

Superstore

TARA PARK CARAVAN SITE

Liverpool to: Douglas (Isle of Man) 2 hrs. 30 mins. (Fast Ferry - Summer only) Douglas (Isle of Man) 4 hrs. (Winter only)

Liverpool to Wallasey (Seacombe Foot Ferry) 7-8 minutes

Birkenhead to Wallasey (Foot Ferry) 10 minutes

Birkenhead to: Belfast 8 hrs. Dublin 7 hrs.

Liverpool to Birkenhead (Woodside Foot Ferry) 7-8 minutes

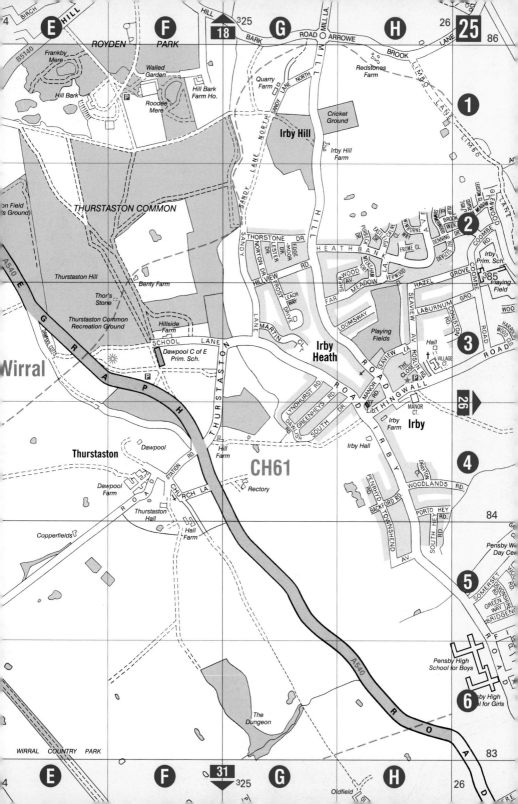

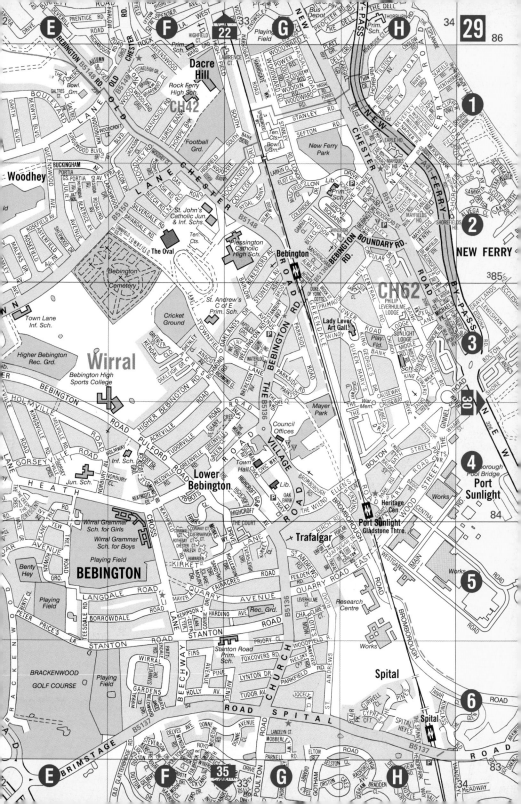

30 34 A B 335 C D 36
▲23

RIVER MERSEY

PAGE NOT CONTINUED

NEW FERRY

Sewage Works

Warehouse

DOCK ROAD NORTH

Works

Factory

Works

Wirral

Bromborough Pool

Cricket Grd.

YORK STREET
MANOR SOUTH
GREEN
Bowl. Grn.
Ten. Cts.

Factory

Bromborough Pool Bridge

Port Sunlight

Works

Court House

OLD COURT HOUSE RD.

SOUTH DOCK

CH62

Works

Works

Warehouse

Factories

Factory

Works

DOCK ROAD SOUTH

Works

Bromborough Port

Works

Depot

CAUSEWAY ROAD

Riverbank

MAGAZINE LANE

Works

GEORGIA AVENUE

Works

Spital

CH63

Spital

Weir

Odeon Cinema

South Wirral Retail Park

Leisure Park

Fitness First

Gala Bingo

Superstore

Works

Works

COMMERCIAL ROAD

Dungeon

▲ 325
25

WIRRAL COUNTRY PARK

Oldfield

Charlcombe

OLDFIELD FARM LA

OLDFIELD DRIVE

• Piper Well

OLDFIELD COTTS

GREENFIELD LA

THE ARBOUR

GREENFIELD LA

OLDFIELD

THE RIDGE

STRATHALLAN CL

OLDFIELD CL

OLDFIELD

OLDFIELD GDNS

DALE GRS

LAUR

WAY

Nursery

Wirral

OLDFIELD

ROAD

FERNS

BROOMFIELD DR

REDSTONE CL

HEATHSIDE

WARREN DRIVE

Dales
Farm

CH60

WIRRAL COUNTRY PARK

BROAD

HILL

RESIDE

ROAD

TARGET

PIPERS

LANE

PIPER'S END

PIPER'S CL

SANDFIELD RD

HATTON CL

82 Hesw
Dale

The Dales

Playing
Field

Holiday
Camp

CROSSLEY DR.

CROFTSWAY

DELAVOR

DALESWAY

ROAD

Sewage
Works

Caravan
/Park

THE MOORINGS

MOSTYN AV

Nursery

CROFTSWAY

DELAVOR

GULLS

TEALS

ROWS WY

DELAVOR CL

LINAO WK.

WY

GUSTS

WAY

32

Slipway

BANKS

WITTERING

P

WEST

LANE

DAL

MARINE DRIVE

PARK

81

MANNERS

SEAFIELD

CLOVERHILL RD

WALL DRIVE

SEABANK

Gayton Hole

380

R I V E R

D E E

1

2

3

4

5

6

TELEGRAPH ROAD

MERE PIN

275

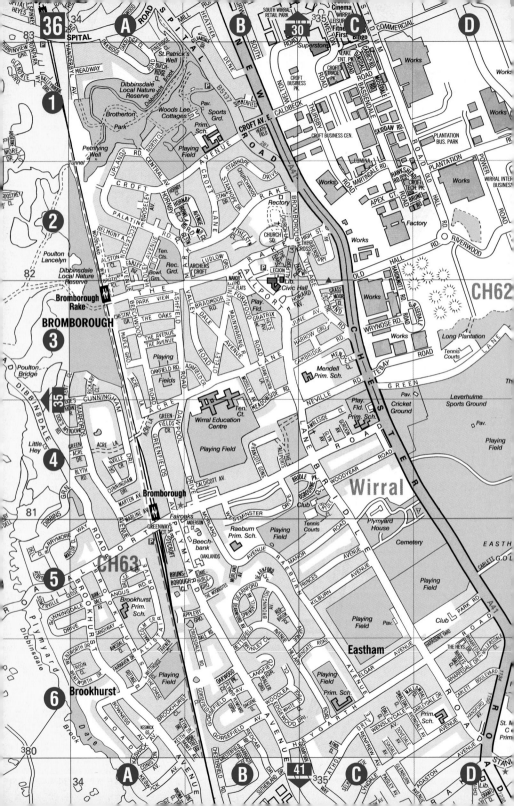

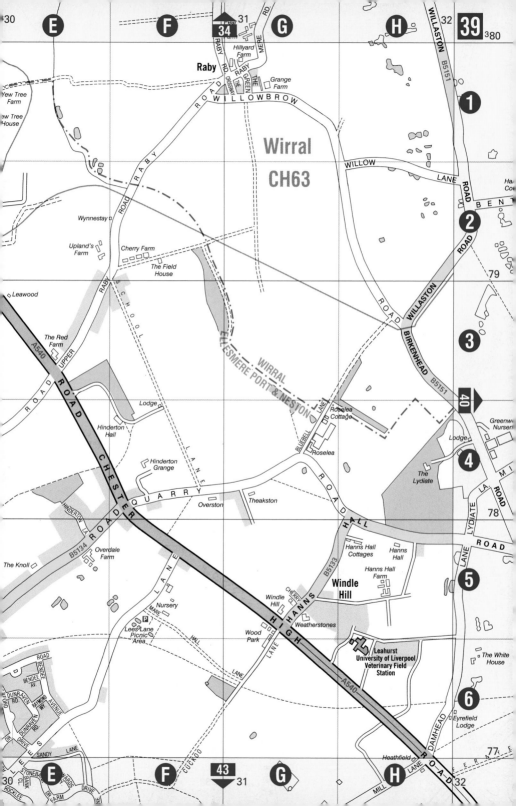

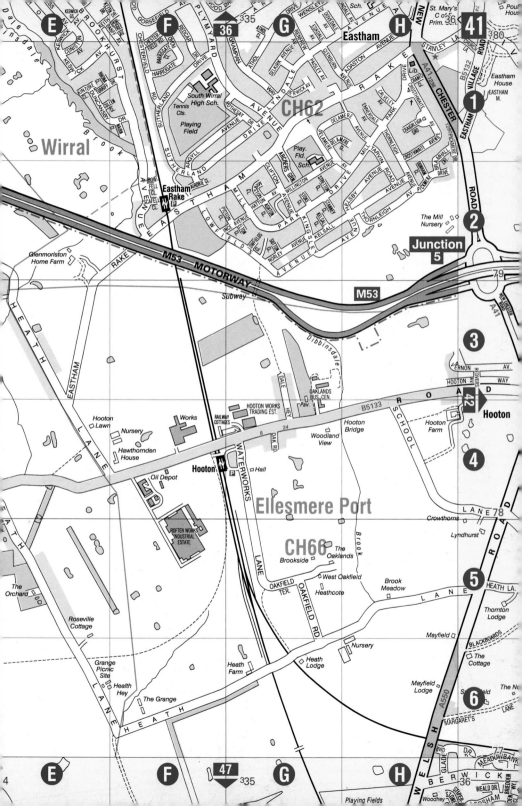

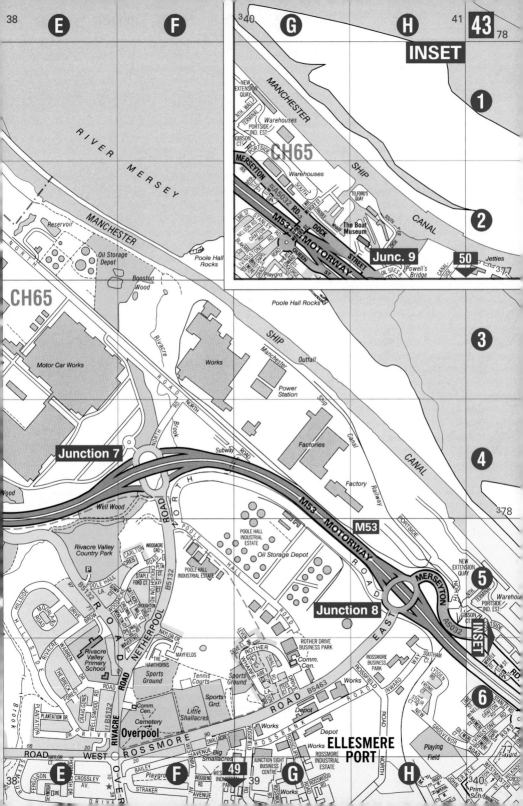

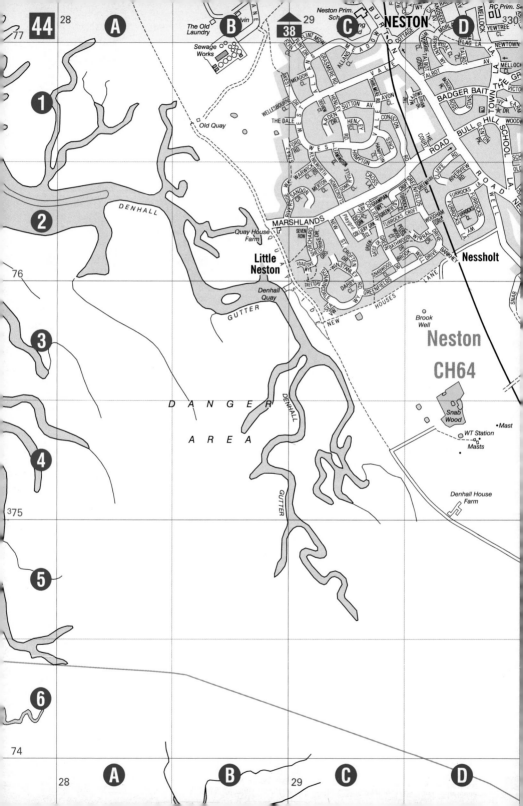

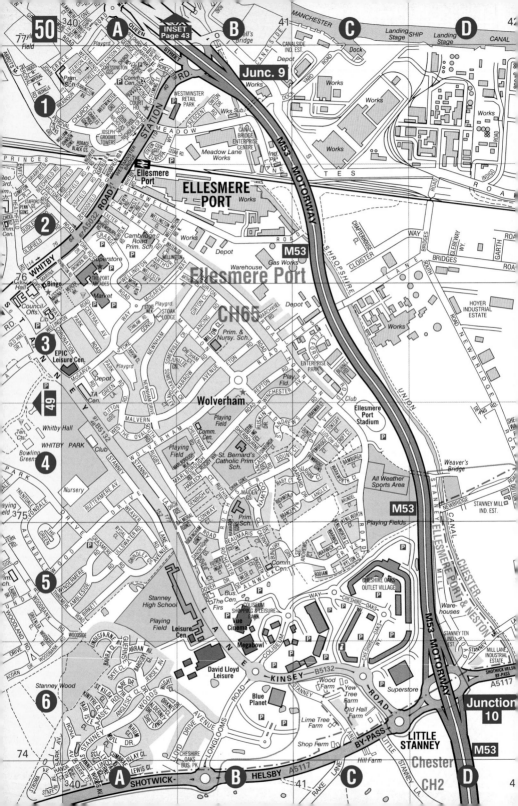

INDEX

Including Streets, Places & Areas, Hospitals & Hospices, Industrial Estates,
Selected Flats & Walkways, Stations, and Selected Places of Interest.

HOW TO USE THIS INDEX

1. Each street name is followed by its Postcode District and then by its Locality abbreviation(s) and then by its map reference;
e.g. **Abbey Rd.** CH48: W Kir . . . .5D **16** is in the CH48 Postcode District and the West Kirby Locality and is to be found in square 5D on page **16**. The page number is shown in bold type.

2. A strict alphabetical order is followed in which Av., Rd., St., etc. (though abbreviated) are read in full and as part of the street name;
e.g. **Abbotsford St.** appears after **Abbots Dr.** but before **Abbots M.**

3. Streets and a selection of flats and walkways too small to be shown on the maps, appear in the index with the thoroughfare to which it is connected shown in brackets; e.g. **Adlington St.** L3: Liv . . . .2F **15** (off Standish St.)

4. Addresses that are in more than one part are referred to as not continuous.

5. Places and areas are shown in the index in **BLUE TYPE** and the map reference is to the actual map square in which the town centre or area is located and not to the place name shown on the map; e.g. **BROMBOROUGH PORT 6C 30**

6. An example of a selected place of interest is Birkenhead Transport Mus. 6B 14

7. An example of a station is **Bankhall Station (Rail)** 3E 7

8. An example of a hospital is ARROWE PARK HOSPITAL 6G 19

GENERAL ABBREVIATIONS

All. : Alley	**Dr.** : Drive	**La.** : Lane	**Shop.** : Shopping
App. : Approach	**E.** : East	**Lit.** : Little	**Sth.** : South
Arc. : Arcade	**Ent.** : Enterprise	**Lwr.** : Lower	**Sq.** : Square
Av. : Avenue	**Est.** : Estate	**Mans.** : Mansions	**Sta.** : Station
Bk. : Back	**Fld.** : Field	**Mkt.** : Market	**St.** : Street
Blvd. : Boulevard	**Flds.** : Fields	**Mdw.** : Meadow	**Ter.** : Terrace
Bri. : Bridge	**Gdn.** : Garden	**M.** : Mews	**Twr.** : Tower
Bldgs. : Buildings	**Gdns.** : Gardens	**Mt.** : Mount	**Trad.** : Trading
Bus. : Business	**Gth.** : Garth	**Mus.** : Museum	**Up.** : Upper
Cvn. : Caravan	**Ga.** : Gate	**Nth.** : North	**Va.** : Vale
C'way. : Causeway	**Gt.** : Great	**Pde.** : Parade	**Vw.** : View
Cen. : Centre	**Grn.** : Green	**Pk.** : Park	**Vs.** : Villas
Cl. : Close	**Gro.** : Grove	**Pas.** : Passage	**Vis.** : Visitors
Comn. : Common	**Hgts.** : Heights	**Pav.** : Pavilion	**Wlk.** : Walk
Cnr. : Corner	**Ho.** : House	**Pl.** : Place	**W.** : West
Cotts. : Cottages	**Ind.** : Industrial	**Pct.** : Precinct	**Yd.** : Yard
Ct. : Court	**Info.** : Information	**Prom.** : Promenade	
Cres. : Crescent	**Intl.** : International	**Ri.** : Rise	
Cft. : Croft	**Junc.** : Junction	**Rd.** : Road	

LOCALITY ABBREVIATIONS

Aig : **Aigburth**	East : **Eastham**	Liv : **Liverpool**	R Ferr : **Rock Ferry**
Back : **Backford**	Ell P : **Ellesmere Port**	Meols : **Meols**	Spit : **Spital**
Barn : **Barnston**	Frank : **Frankby**	More : **Moreton**	Stoak : **Stoak**
Beb : **Bebington**	Grea : **Greasby**	Ness : **Ness**	Store : **Storeton**
Bid : **Bidston**	Gt Sut : **Great Sutton**	Nest : **Neston**	Thing : **Thingwall**
Birk : **Birkenhead**	Hes : **Heswall**	New B : **New Brighton**	Thorn H : **Thornton Hough**
Boot : **Bootle**	High B : **Higher Bebington**	New F : **New Ferry**	Thurs : **Thurstaston**
Brim : **Brimstage**	Hoot : **Hooton**	Noct : **Noctorum**	Tran : **Tranmere**
Brom : **Bromborough**	Hoy : **Hoylake**	O'ton : **Oxton**	Upton : **Upton**
Burt : **Burton**	Irby : **Irby**	Park : **Parkgate**	Wall : **Wallasey**
Caldy : **Caldy**	Kirk : **Kirkdale**	Pens : **Pensby**	Walt : **Walton**
Cap : **Capenhurst**	Leas : **Leasowe**	Port S : **Port Sunlight**	W Kir : **West Kirby**
Chil T : **Childer Thornton**	Led : **Ledsham**	Pren : **Prenton**	Whit : **Whitby**
Chor B : **Chorlton-by-Backford**	Lit N : **Little Neston**	Pudd : **Puddington**	Will : **Willaston**
C'ton : **Claughton**	Lit Stan : **Little Stanney**	Raby : **Raby**	W'bnk : **Woodbank**
Dunk : **Dunkirk**	Lit Sut : **Little Sutton**	Raby M : **Raby Mere**	W'chu : **Woodchurch**

A

A41 Expressway
CH42: Tran 4B 22
Abbey Cl. CH41: Birk 2B 22
Abbeyfield Ho. CH65: Whit . .4G 49
Abbey Rd. CH48: W Kir 5D 16
Abbey St. CH41: Birk 2B 22
Abbot Cl. CH43: Bid 1A 20
Abbots Dr. CH63: Beb 4F 29
Abbotsford St. CH44: Wall . . .3A 14
Abbots M. CH65: Ell P 1H 49
Abbots Way CH48: W Kir . . .4E 17
CH64: Nest 5C 38
Abercromby Sq. L7: Liv 4H 15
(not continuous)

Aberdeen St. CH41: Birk 6G 13
Aberford Av. CH45: Wall 6C 4
Aber St. L6: Liv 2H 15
Abingdon Rd.
CH49: Grea 4B 18
Abram St. L5: Liv 6G 7
Acacia Cl. CH49: Grea 6C 18
Acacia Dr. CH66: Gt Sut 6F 49
Acacia Gro. CH44: Wall 3A 14
CH48: W Kir 5C 16
Ackers Rd. CH49: W'chu 5A 20
Acland Rd. CH44: Wall 1F 13
Acorn Cl. CH63: High B 3D 28
Acorn Ct. L8: Liv 1G 23
Acorn Dr. CH65: Whit 6H 49
Acrefield Ct. CH42: Tran 6F 21
Acrefield Rd. CH42: Tran 6F 21

Acre La. CH60: Hes 2E 33
CH62: Brom 4A 36
CH63: Brom 4A 36
Acre Rd. CH66: Gt Sut 2D 48
Acres Rd. CH47: Meols 6H 9
CH63: Beb 3F 29
Acreville Rd. CH63: Beb 4F 29
Acton La. CH46: More 6C 10
Acton Rd. CH42: R Ferr 6C 22
Acuba Gro. CH42: Tran 3A 22
Adam Av. CH66: Gt Sut 3C 48
(not continuous)
Adam Cl. CH66: Gt Sut 3D 48
Adam St. L5: Liv 5H 7
Adaston Av. CH62: East 1H 41
Addington St. CH44: Wall 2H 13
Addison St. L3: Liv 2F 15

Addison Way L3: Liv 2F 15
Adelaide Pl. L5: Liv 1G 15
Adelaide Rd. CH42: Tran 3G 21
Adelaide St. CH44: Wall 2F 13
Adelphi St. CH41: Birk 1A 22
Adkins St. L5: Liv 5H 7
Adlington Ho. L3: Liv 2F 15
Adlington St. L3: Liv 2F 15
(off Standish St.)
Admiral Gro. L8: Liv 1H 23
Admiral St. L8: Liv 2H 23
Agnes Gro. CH44: Wall 6G 5
Agnes Jones Ho. L8: Liv 5H 15
Agnes Rd. CH42: Tran 4H 21
Aigburth Gro. CH46: More . . .5D 10
Ailsa Rd. CH45: Wall 6E 5

Bk. Berry St.—Bentfield Cl.

Bk. Berry St. L1: Liv 5G **15**
Bk. Blackfield Ter. L4: Kirk 4F **7**
Bk. Bold St. L1: Liv 4G **15**
Bk. Boundary Cl. L5: Kirk 5F **7**
Bk. Bridport St. *L3: Liv 3G 15*
(off Bridport St.)
Bk. Canning St. L8: Liv 5G **15**
Bk. Catharine St. L8: Liv 5H **15**
Bk. Chadwick Mt. L5: Liv 4G **7**
Bk. Colquitt St. L1: Liv 5F **15**
Bk. Commutation Row
L3: Liv 3G **15**
Bk. Egerton St. Nth.
L8: Liv 6H **15**
Bk. Egerton St. Sth.
L8: Liv 6H **15**
Bk. Falkner St. Sth.
L8: Liv 5H **15**
Backford Cl. CH43: O'ton 4C **20**
Backford Gdns. CH1: Back 6A **48**
Backford Rd. CH61: Irby 4H **25**
Bk. Granton Rd. L5: Liv 5H **7**
Bk. Guilford St. L6: Liv 1H **15**
Bk. Hope Pl. L1: Liv 5G **15**
Bk. Huskisson St. L8: Liv 6H **15**
Bk. Knight St. L1: Liv 5G **15**
Bk. Langham St. L4: Walt 3H **7**
Bk. Leeds St. L3: Liv 2D **14**
Bk. Lime St. *L1: Liv 4F 15*
(off Lime St.)
Back Lit. Canning St.
L8: Liv 6H **15**
Bk. Lord St. L1: Liv 4E **15**
Bk. Luton Gro. *L4: Walt 3G 7*
(off Walton Rd.)
Bk. Maryland St. L1: Liv 5G **15**
Bk. Menai St. CH41: Birk 1G **21**
Back Mt. Vernon Vw.
L7: Liv 3H **15**
Bk. Mulberry St. L7: Liv 5H **15**
Bk. Oliver St. CH41: Birk 1A **22**
Bk. Percy St. L8: Liv 6H **15**
Bk. Pickop St. L3: Liv 2E **15**
Bk. Price St. CH41: Birk 6H **13**
Bk. Renshaw St. L1: Liv 4G **15**
Bk. Rockfield Rd. L4: Walt 4H **7**
Bk. St Bride St. L8: Liv 5H **15**
Bk. Sandon St. L8: Liv 6H **15**
Bk. Seaview CH47: Hoy 6D **8**
Bk. Seel St. L1: Liv 5F **15**
Bk. Sir Howard St.
L8: Liv 5H **15**
Bk. Westminster Rd.
L4: Kirk 3G **7**
Bk. York Ter. L5: Liv 5G **7**
Bader Cl. CH61: Pens 6B **26**
Badger Bait CH64: Lit N 1D **44**
Badgers Cl. CH66: Gt Sut 6A **48**
Badgers Pk. CH64: Lit N 1D **44**
Badgersrake La.
CH66: Led 4E **47**
Badger's Set CH48: Caldy 3B **24**
Badger Way CH43: Pren 1G **27**
Badminton St.
L8: Liv 4H **23**
Baffin Cl. CH46: Leas 1G **11**
Bagnall St. L4: Walt 4H **7**
Baildon Grn.
CH66: Lit Sut 1B **48**
Bailey Av. CH65: Ell P 1F **49**
Bailey St. L1: Liv 5F **15**
Baker Dr. CH66: Gt Sut 4E **49**
Baker St. L6: Liv 2H **15**
Baker Way L6: Liv 2H **15**
Bala Gro. CH44: Wall 2E **13**
Balfour Rd. CH43: O'ton 2F **21**
CH44: Wall 2E **13**
Balfour St. L4: Walt 4H **7**
Ballantyne Dr. CH43: Bid 4A **12**
Ballantyne Wlk.
CH43: Bid 4A **12**
Ballard Rd. CH48: W Kir 4G **17**
Ball Av. CH45: New B 3E **5**
Balliol Cl. CH43: Bid 4A **12**
Balliol Ho. L20: Boot 1E **7**
Balliol Rd. L20: Boot 1E **7**
Balliol Rd. E. L20: Boot 1F **7**
Ball's Rd. CH43: O'ton 3F **21**
Balls Rd. E. CH41: Birk 2G **21**
Balmoral Gdns.
CH43: Pren 6D **20**
CH65: Ell P 4B **50**
Balmoral Gro. CH43: Noct 4B **20**
Balmoral Rd. CH45: New B 2G **5**
Baltic St. L4: Walt 4H **7**
Baltimore St. L1: Liv 5G **15**
Bamburgh Ct. CH65: Ell P 4C **50**
Banbury Way CH43: O'ton 5C **20**
Banff Av. CH63: East 6B **36**
Bangor Cl. CH66: Gt Sut 6A **48**
Bangor Rd. CH45: Wall 5B **4**
Bangor St. L5: Liv 6E **7**
Bank Cl. CH64: Lit N 1E **45**
Bank Dene CH42: R Ferr 1G **29**
Bankfields Dr. CH62: East 6F **37**
Bankfield St. L20: Kirk 3D **6**
Bankhall La. L20: Kirk 3E **7**
Bankhall Station (Rail) **3E 7**
Bankhall St. L20: Kirk 3E **7**
Bankhey CH64: Lit N 2D **44**
Banks, The CH45: Wall 4C **4**
Bank's Av. CH47: Meols 5F **9**
Bankside Rd.
CH42: R Ferr 1F **29**
Banks Rd. CH48: W Kir 5C **16**
CH60: Hes 4H **31**
Bank St. CH41: Birk 1A **22**
Bankville Rd. CH42: Tran 4H **21**
Banning Cl. CH41: Birk 6H **13**
Barberry Cl. CH46: More 5B **10**
Barclay St. L8: Liv 3H **23**
Barcombe Rd. CH60: Hes 2F **33**
Bardsay Rd. L4: Walt 2H **7**
Bardsey Cl. CH65: Ell P 6A **50**
Barford Cl. CH43: Bid 1H **19**
Barford Grange
CH64: Will 5D **40**
Barker La. CH49: Grea 5C **18**
(not continuous)
Barker Rd. CH61: Irby 3B **26**
Barkis Cl. L8: Liv 2H **23**
Barleyfield CH61: Pens 5B **26**
Barleymow Cl.
CH66: Gt Sut 5C **48**
Barlow Av. CH63: Beb 3G **29**
Barlow La. L4: Kirk 3G **7**
Barlow St. L4: Kirk 3G **7**
Barmouth Rd. CH45: Wall 5B **4**
Barmouth Way L5: Liv 5E **7**
Barnacre Dr. CH64: Park 3A **38**
Barnacre La. CH46: More 1C **18**
Barnard Dr. CH65: Ell P 4C **50**
Barnard Rd. CH43: O'ton 2F **21**
Barncroft, The
CH49: Grea 3D **18**
Barnes Grn. CH63: Spit 1G **35**
Barnfield Cl. CH47: Meols 4G **9**
CH66: Gt Sut 5C **48**
Barn Hey CH47: Hoy 2C **16**
Barn Hey Cres.
CH47: Meols 5H **9**
Barnsdale Av.
CH61: Thing 4D **26**
BARNSTON **5E 27**
Barnston Av. CH65: Ell P 2F **49**
Barnston La. CH46: More 4E **11**
Barnston Rd. CH60: Hes 4D **32**
CH61: Barn, Thing 2D **26**
Barnston Towers Cl.
CH60: Hes 3E **33**
Barnwell Av. CH44: Wall 6F **5**
Barnwood CH66: Lit Sut 6H **41**
Barren Gro. CH43: O'ton 3F **21**
Barrington Rd.
CH44: Wall 2G **13**
Barr St. L20: Kirk 3E **7**
Barry Cl. CH65: Ell P 6A **50**
Barrymore Way
CH63: Brom 5H **35**
Barton Cl. CH47: Hoy 1B **16**
Barton Hey Dr.
CH48: Caldy 3A **24**
Barton Rd. CH47: Hoy 1B **16**
Barton St. CH41: Birk 1G **21**
CH43: O'ton 2G **21**
Baskervyle Cl. CH60: Hes 5C **32**
Baskervyle Rd.
CH60: Hes 5C **32**
Basnett St. L1: Liv 4F **15**
Bassendale Rd.
CH62: Brom 1C **36**
Bassenthwaite Av.
CH43: Noct 2B **20**
Bath St. CH62: Port S 4H **29**
L3: Liv 3D **14**
Bathwood Dr. CH64: Lit N 2C **44**
Baumville Dr. CH63: Spit 1F **35**
Bayhorse La. L3: Liv 3H **15**
Baysdale Cl. L8: Liv 3H **23**
Bayswater Ct. CH45: Wall 5B **4**
Bayswater Gdns. CH45: Wall . . .4B **4**
Bayswater Rd. CH45: Wall 5B **4**
Baytree Cl. CH66: Gt Sut 6F **49**
Baytree Rd. CH42: Tran 4A **22**
CH48: Frank 5H **17**
Bay Vw. Dr. CH45: Wall 4B **4**
Beachcroft Rd.
CH47: Meols 4G **9**
Beach Gro. CH45: Wall 4G **5**
Beach Rd. CH47: Hoy 1B **16**
Beach Wlk. CH48: W Kir 1A **24**
Beacon Ct. CH60: Hes 3C **32**
Beacon Dr. CH48: W Kir 5E **17**
Beacon Ho. L5: Liv 1G **15**
Beacon La. CH60: Hes 3C **32**
L5: Liv 5H **7**
Beacon Pde. CH60: Hes 3C **32**
Beacons, The CH60: Hes 4C **32**
Beaconsfield Cl.
CH42: Tran 4A **22**
Beaconsfield Rd.
CH62: New F 2H **29**
Beasley Cl. CH66: Gt Sut 4D **48**
Beatles Story, The **5E 15**
Beatrice Av. CH63: High B 2E **29**
Beatrice St. L20: Boot 2F **7**
Beatty Cl. CH48: Caldy 3A **24**
Beaufort Dr. CH44: Wall 6C **4**
Beaufort Rd. CH41: Birk 4D **12**
Beaufort St. L8: Liv 1G **23**
(Hill St.)
L8: Liv 2G **23**
(Northumberland St.)
L8: Liv 1G **23**
(Stanhope St.)
Beau La. L3: Liv 1G **15**
Beaumaris Ct.
CH43: O'ton 2F **21**
Beaumaris Dr.
CH61: Thing 3D **26**
CH65: Ell P 5B **50**
Beaumaris Rd.
CH45: Wall 5B **4**
Beaumaris St. L20: Kirk 3D **6**
(not continuous)
Beau St. L3: Liv 1G **15**
Beauworth Av. CH49: Grea . . .4C **18**
BEBINGTON **5F 29**
Bebington Rd. CH42: Tran 5H **21**
CH62: New F 2G **29**
CH63: Beb 3G **29**
CH66: Gt Sut 3D **48**
Bebington Station (Rail) **2G 29**
Beckenham Rd.
CH45: New B 2F **5**
Becket St. L4: Kirk 3F **7**
(not continuous)
Beckett Gro.
CH63: High B 2D **28**
Beckwith St. CH41: Birk 5F **13**
L1: Liv 5E **15**
Beckwith St. E.
CH41: Birk 6H **13**
Bedford Av. CH42: R Ferr 6A **22**
CH65: Whit 5G **49**
Bedford Av. E.
CH65: Whit 5H **49**
Bedford Cl. L7: Liv 5H **15**
Bedford Ct. CH42: R Ferr 5B **22**
Bedford Dr. CH42: R Ferr 6H **21**
Bedford Pl. CH42: R Ferr 5C **22**
L20: Boot 2D **6**
Bedford Rd. CH42: R Ferr 5B **22**
CH45: Wall 5F **5**
L20: Boot 2E **7**
Bedford Rd. E.
CH42: R Ferr 5C **22**
Bedford St. Nth. L7: Liv 4H **15**
Bedford St. Sth. L7: Liv 5H **15**
(not continuous)
Bedford Wlk. L7: Liv 5H **15**
Beech Av. CH49: Upton 1D **18**
CH61: Pens 5C **26**
Beech Ct. CH42: Tran 3H **21**
Beechcroft Dr.
CH65: Whit 4H **49**
Beechcroft Rd.
CH44: Wall 3G **13**
Beeches, The
CH42: R Ferr 6B **22**
CH46: Leas 2E **11**
CH66: Gt Sut 3D **48**
Beechfield Cl. CH60: Hes 4C **32**
Beechfield Rd.
CH65: Ell P 2H **49**
Beech Gro. CH66: Whit 6B **48**
Beech Hey La. CH64: Will 4D **40**
Beech Lodge CH43: Noct 2B **20**
Beech Rd. CH42: Tran 3G **21**
CH60: Hes 3E **33**
CH63: High B 2F **29**
Beechway CH63: Beb 6F **29**
Beechways Dr.
CH64: Nest 6B **38**
BEECHWOOD **5A 12**
Beechwood Av. CH45: Wall 6C **4**
Beechwood Ct.
CH49: W'chu 6H **19**
Beechwood Dr. CH43: Bid 6A **12**
CH66: Gt Sut 6D **48**
Beechwood Recreation Cen.
. . . .**6H 11**
Beechwood Rd.
CH62: Brom 3A **36**
Beeston Cl. CH43: Bid 1A **20**
Beeston Dr. CH61: Pens 5B **26**
Beeston Grn.
CH66: Gt Sut 2E **49**
Beeston St. L4: Kirk 2G **7**
Beetham Plaza *L2: Liv 4E 15*
(off Brunswick St.)
Belfield Dr. CH43: O'ton 4F **21**
Belford Dr. CH46: More 5B **10**
Belfry Cl. CH46: More 4B **10**
Belgrave Av. CH44: Wall 1G **13**
Belgrave Dr. CH65: Ell P 2F **49**
Belgrave St. CH44: Wall 6F **5**
Bellamy Rd. L4: Walt 1G **7**
Belldene Gro. CH61: Hes 1B **32**
Belle Vue Rd. CH44: Wall 3H **13**
Bellfield Cres.
CH45: New B 3E **5**
Bell Rd. CH44: Wall 2H **13**
Belltower Rd. L20: Kirk 4D **6**
Bellward Cl. CH63: Spit 1F **35**
Belmont CH41: Birk 2G **21**
Belmont Av. CH62: Brom 2A **36**
Belmont Dr. CH61: Pens 6C **26**
Belmont Gro. CH43: O'ton 2G **21**
Belmont Rd. CH45: New B 2F **5**
CH48: W Kir 4D **16**
Beloe St. L8: Liv 3H **23**
Belvedere Ct.
CH49: W'chu 6H 19
(off Childwall Grn.)
Belvidere Rd. CH45: Wall 5D **4**
Benbow Cl. CH43: Bid 5D **12**
Benbow St. L20: Boot 1D **6**
Bendee Av. CH64: Lit N 6E **39**
Bendee Rd. CH64: Lit N 6D **38**
Benedict Ct. L20: Boot 2E **7**
Benedict St. L20: Boot 2F **7**
Bengel St. L7: Liv 3H **15**
Benledi St. L5: Liv 6F **7**
Bennet's La. CH47: Meols 3G **9**
Bennett Cl. CH64: Will 5C **40**
Bennetts Hill CH43: O'ton 3F **21**
Bennett Wlk. CH61: Pens 6B **26**
Ben Nevis Dr.
CH66: Lit Sut 1H **47**
Ben Nevis Rd.
CH42: Tran 5H **21**
Benson Cl. CH49: Upton 3F **19**
Benson St. L1: Liv 4G **15**
Bentfield Cl.
CH63: High B 2D **28**

Bentfield Gdns.—Bramhall Dr.

Bentfield Gdns.
CH63: High B 2D **28**
Bentham Cl. CH43: Noct 4C **20**
Bentinck Cl. CH41: Birk 1G **21**
Bentinck Pl. CH41: Birk 1G **21**
Bentinck St. CH41: Birk 1G **21**
(not continuous)
L5: Liv 6D **6**
Bentley Rd. CH43: O'ton 3F **21**
CH61: Pens 4B **26**
Benton Cl. L5: Liv 5F **7**
Bent Way CH60: Hes 2C **32**
Benty Cl. CH63: High B 5E **29**
Benty Farm Gro.
CH61: Pens 4C **26**
Benty Heath La.
CH64: Will 2A **40**
CH66: Hoot 2D **40**
Beresford Av. CH63: Beb 2G **29**
Beresford Cl. CH43: O'ton 2E **21**
Beresford Ct. CH43: O'ton 2E **21**
Beresford Rd.
CH43: O'ton 2D **20**
CH45: Wall 4D **4**
L8: Liv 3H **23**
Beresford St. L5: Liv 1G **15**
L20: Boot 2D **6**
Berey's Bldgs. *L3: Liv 3E 15*
(off Bixteth St.)
Bergen Cl. L20: Boot 1G **7**
Berkeley Av. CH43: Pren 6D **20**
Berkeley Ct. *CH49: W'chu 6G 19*
(off Childwall Grn.)
Berkeley Dr. CH45: New B 4G **5**
Berkley Cl. L8: Liv 1H **23**
Berkley St. L8: Liv 6H **15**
Bermuda Rd. CH46: More 4C **10**
Bernard Av. CH45: New B 4G **5**
Berner St. CH41: Birk 5H **13**
Berry Cl. CH66: Gt Sut 4C **48**
Berry Dr. CH66: Gt Sut 3C **48**
Berrylands Cl. CH46: More 4D **10**
Berrylands Rd.
CH46: More 3D **10**
Berry St. L1: Liv 5G **15**
L20: Boot 1D **6**
Berry St. Ind. Est.
L20: Boot 1D **6**
Bertha Gdns. CH41: Birk 5D **12**
Bertha St. CH41: Birk 5D **12**
Bertram Dr. CH47: Meols 5E **9**
Bertram Dr. Nth.
CH47: Meols 5F **9**
Berwick Av. CH62: East 1G **41**
Berwick Cl. CH43: Bid 1A **20**
CH46: More 5B **10**
Berwick Gdns.
CH66: Lit Sut 1B **48**
Berwick Gro.
CH66: Lit Sut 1B **48**
Berwick Rd.
CH66: Lit Sut 1H **47**
Berwyn Av. CH47: Hoy 6E **9**
CH61: Thing 3C **26**
Berwyn Blvd.
CH63: High B 1E **29**
Berwyn Cl. CH66: Lit Sut 1A **48**
Berwyn Dr. CH61: Hes 1C **32**
Berwyn Rd. CH44: Wall 6G **5**
Beryl Rd. CH43: Noct 2A **20**
Bessborough Rd.
CH43: O'ton 3F **21**
Bessemer St. L8: Liv 3H **23**
Beta Cl. CH62: New F 2G **29**
Bethany Cres. CH63: Beb 4F **29**
Bettisfield Av.
CH62: Brom 6B **36**
Beverley Dr. CH60: Hes 5D **32**
Beverley Gdns.
CH61: Thing 3D **26**
Beverley Rd. CH45: Wall 5D **4**
CH62: New F 1H **29**
Beverley Way
CH66: Lit Sut 6B **42**
Bevington Bush L3: Liv 2F **15**
Bevington Hill L3: Liv 1F **15**
Bevington St. L3: Liv 1F **15**
Bevyl Rd. CH64: Park 3A **38**
Bewey Cl. L8: Liv 3G **23**
Bianca St. L20: Boot 2E **7**
Bickerstaffe St. L3: Liv 2G **15**
Bickerton Av.
CH63: High B 1D **28**
Bidder St. L3: Liv 2G **15**
Bidson Link Rd.
CH44: Wall 3B **12**
BIDSTON 5B **12**
Bidston Av. CH41: Birk 6D **12**
CH45: Wall 5C **4**
Bidston Ct. CH43: Noct 6C **12**
Bidston Grn.
CH66: Gt Sut 3D **48**
Bidston Grn. Ct.
CH43: Bid 5A **12**
Bidston Grn. Dr.
CH43: Bid 5A **12**
Bidston Ind. Est.
CH44: Wall 2B **12**
Bidston Link Rd.
CH43: Bid 3B **12**
Bidston Moss CH44: Wall 2B **12**
Bidston Moss Nature Reserve
2C **12**
Bidston Rd.
CH43: C'ton, O'ton 1C **20**
Bidston Sta. App.
CH43: Bid 3A **12**
Bidston Station (Rail) 3A **12**
Bidston Vw. CH43: Bid 4A **12**
Bidston Village Rd.
CH43: Bid 4H **11**
Big Mdw. Rd.
CH49: W'chu 3G **19**
Billings Cl. L5: Kirk 5E **7**
Binsey Cl. CH49: Upton 2D **18**
Birchall St. L20: Kirk 4E **7**
Birch Av. CH49: Upton 1D **18**
Birch Cl. CH43: O'ton 4F **21**
Birch Ct. *L8: Liv 3H 23*
(off Weller Way)
Birchdale Cl. CH49: Grea 2D **18**
Birches, The CH44: Wall 3A **14**
CH64: Nest 3D **38**
Birches Cl. CH60: Hes 3C **32**
Birchfield CH46: More 6C **10**
Birchfield Cl. CH46: More 6C **10**
Birchfield Rd. L4: Walt 1H **7**
Birchfield St. L3: Liv 2G **15**
Birch Gro. CH45: New B 4G **5**
CH66: Whit 6G **49**
Birch Heys CH48: Frank 6A **18**
Birchmere CH60: Hes 1A **32**
Birchridge Cl. CH62: Spit 1A **36**
Birch Rd. CH43: O'ton 4F **21**
CH47: Meols 5G **9**
CH63: Beb 5G **29**
Birch St. L5: Liv 6D **6**
Birchview Way
CH43: Noct 2B **20**
Birchway CH60: Hes 6E **33**
Birchwood Av. CH41: Birk 6H **13**
Birchwood Cl. CH41: Birk 6H **13**
CH66: Gt Sut 6D **48**
Birkdale Av. CH63: Brom 5A **36**
BIRKENHEAD 1B **22**
Birkenhead Central Station (Rail)
2A **22**
Birkenhead North Station (Rail)
4D **12**
Birkenhead Park Station (Rail)
5F **13**
Birkenhead Priory 1B **22**
Birkenhead Rd.
CH44: Wall 4A **14**
CH47: Hoy, Meols 5E **9**
CH64: Will 3H **39**
Birkenhead Transport Mus.
6B **14**
Birket Av. CH46: Leas 2F **11**
Birket Cl. CH46: Leas 2G **11**
Birket Ho. CH41: Birk 6H **13**
Birket Sq. CH46: Leas 2G **11**
Birkett Av. CH65: Ell P 5A **50**
Birkett Rd. CH42: R Ferr 6A **22**
CH48: W Kir 3D **16**
Birkett St. L3: Liv 2G **15**
Birley Ct. L8: Liv 6H **15**
Birnam Rd. CH44: Wall 2H **13**
Bishop Rd. CH44: Wall 3F **13**
Bishops Ct. CH43: O'ton 4E **21**
Bishops Gdns.
CH65: Ell P 2G **49**
Bishop Sheppard Ct.
L3: Liv 1E **15**
Bisley St. CH45: Wall 6F **5**
Bispham Dr. CH47: Meols 6G **9**
Bispham Ho. L3: Liv 2F **15**
Bixteth St. L3: Liv 3E **15**
Blackboards La.
CH66: Chil T 6A **42**
Blackburne Pl. L8: Liv 5H **15**
Blackburne Ter. L8: Liv 5H **15**
Blackdown Cl.
CH66: Lit Sut 2A **48**
Blackeys La. CH64: Nest 5C **38**
Blackfield St. L5: Kirk 5F **7**
Blackheath Dr.
CH46: Leas 2F **11**
Black Horse Cl.
CH48: W Kir 4E **17**
Black Horse Hill
CH48: W Kir 5E **17**
Black Lion La.
CH66: Lit Sut 1B **48**
Blackpool St. CH41: Birk 2A **22**
Blackstock St. L3: Liv 2E **15**
Blackstone St. L5: Liv 5D **6**
Blackthorne Av.
CH66: Whit 6B **48**
Blackthorne Cl.
CH46: More 6F **11**
Blair Ct. CH43: C'ton 1E **21**
Blair Pk. CH63: Spit 6H **29**
Blair St. L8: Liv 6G **15**
Blakeley Brow
CH63: Raby M 5G **35**
Blakeley Ct.
CH63: Raby M 5G **35**
Blakeley Dell
CH63: Raby M 5H **35**
Blakeley Dene
CH63: Raby M 4H **35**
Blakeley Rd.
CH63: Raby M 4G **35**
Blakemere Ct.
CH65: Ell P 2G **43**
Blakeney Cl. CH49: Upton 6G **11**
Blakenhall Way
CH49: Upton 1D **18**
Blaydon Wlk. CH43: C'ton 1C **20**
Bleasdale Cl.
CH49: Upton 1E **19**
Blenheim Rd. CH44: Wall 6H **5**
Blenheim St. L5: Liv 6E **7**
Blessington Rd. L4: Walt 4H **7**
Bletchley Av. CH44: Wall 1D **12**
Bluebell Av. CH41: Birk 5D **12**
Bluebell La. CH64: Nest 4G **39**
Bluecoat Arts Cen. 4F **15**
Bluecoat Chambers
L1: Liv 4F 15
(off School La.)
Bluecoat Display Cen. 4F **15**
Bluefields St. L8: Liv 6H **15**
Blue Planet 6B **50**
Bluewood Dr. CH41: Birk 4B **12**
Blundells Dr. CH46: More 4F **11**
Blundell St. L1: Liv 6F **15**
Blyth Rd. CH63: Brom 4A **36**
Boathouse La.
CH64: Park 3A **38**
Boat Mus., The 2H **43**
Bob Paisley Ct. L5: Liv 5H **7**
Bodiam Ct. CH65: Ell P 5C **50**
Bodley St. L4: Walt 4H **7**
Bodmin Rd. L4: Walt 2H **7**
Bolde Way CH63: Spit 2G **35**
Bold Pl. L1: Liv 5G **15**
Bold St. L1: Liv 4F **15**
Bollington Cl.
CH43: O'ton 4D **20**
Bolton Rd. CH62: Port S 4H **29**
Bolton Rd. E.
CH62: Port S 3A **30**
Bolton St. L3: Liv 4F **15**
Bond St. L3: Liv 1F **15**
BOOTLE 1F **7**
Bootle Oriel Road Station (Rail)
1D **6**
Border Rd. CH60: Hes 3D **32**
Border Way L5: Liv 5G **7**
Borough Pavement
CH41: Birk 1H **21**
Borough Pl. CH41: Birk 1A **22**
Borough Rd. CH41: Birk 4G **21**
CH42: Tran 4G **21**
CH44: Wall 2H **13**
Borough Rd. E.
CH41: Birk 1A **22**
(not continuous)
CH44: Wall 3A **14**
Borough Way CH44: Wall 3A **14**
Borrowdale Rd.
CH46: More 5D **10**
CH63: Beb 5E **29**
Bosnia St. L8: Liv 4H **23**
Bostock Grn. CH65: Ell P 1F **49**
Bostock St. L5: Liv 6F **7**
Boswell Rd. CH43: Pren 6D **20**
Bosworth Cl. CH63: Spit 1F **35**
Botley Cl. CH49: Upton 2D **18**
Boulevard, The
CH65: Gt Sut 2F **49**
L8: Liv 1H **23**
Boulton Av. CH48: W Kir 3D **16**
CH62: New F 1H **29**
Boundary La. CH60: Hes 3C **32**
Boundary Pk. CH64: Park 6B **38**
Boundary Rd. CH43: Bid 4B **12**
CH48: W Kir 1B **24**
CH62: Port S 2H **29**
Boundary St. L5: Liv 5D **6**
Boundary St. E. L5: Liv 5F **7**
Bousfield St. L4: Walt 4G **7**
Bowdon Rd. CH45: Wall 5E **5**
Bower Ho. CH49: Upton 6F **11**
Bower Rd. CH60: Hes 4E **33**
Bowfell Cl. CH62: East 2F **41**
Bowgreen Cl. CH43: Bid 6A **12**
Bowland Cl. CH62: Brom 2A **36**
Bowness Av. CH43: Pren 5E **21**
CH63: Brom 6A **36**
Bowood St. L8: Liv 4H **23**
Bowring Dr. CH64: Park 4A **38**
Bowring St. L8: Liv 3H **23**
Bowscale Cl.
CH49: Upton 2E **19**
Boyd Cl. CH46: Leas 2H **11**
Brackendale CH49: W'chu 4A **20**
Bracken Dr. CH48: W Kir 5G **17**
Brackenhurst Dr.
CH45: New B 4G **5**
Bracken La. CH63: High B 4D **28**
Bracken Rd. CH66: Gt Sut 3E **49**
Brackenside CH60: Hes 1B **32**
Brackenwood Rd.
CH63: High B 6E **29**
Brackley Cl. CH44: Wall 2E **13**
Bradda Cl. CH49: Upton 6F **11**
Bradden Cl. CH63: Spit 1H **35**
Bradewell Cl. L4: Kirk 3G **7**
Bradewell St. L4: Kirk 3G **7**
Bradgate Cl. CH46: More 4B **10**
Bradman Cl. CH45: Wall 6F **5**
Bradman Rd. CH46: More 4C **10**
Bradmoor Rd. CH62: Brom 3B **36**
Bradwall Cl. CH65: Whit 3G **49**
Bradwell Cl. CH48: W Kir 5F **17**
Braehaven Rd.
CH45: New B 4G **5**
Braemar Ct. CH65: Ell P 4C **50**
Braemar St. L20: Kirk 2F **7**
Braemore Rd. CH44: Wall 1D **12**
Braeside Cl. CH66: Gt Sut 2C **48**
Braeside Gdns.
CH49: Upton 2F **19**
Braid St. CH41: Birk 5H **13**
Bramble Av. CH41: Birk 5D **12**
Bramble Way CH46: More 3D **10**
Bramblewood Cl.
CH43: Noct 3B **20**
Bramerton Ct.
CH48: W Kir 4C **16**
Bramford Cl. CH49: Upton 2E **19**
Bramhall Cl. CH48: W Kir 6F **17**
Bramhall Dr. CH62: East 2H **41**

Bramley Av.—Bush Way

Bramley Av. CH63: High B 2E **29**
Bramley Cl. CH66: Gt Sut 6A **48**
Brampton Dr. L8: Liv 5H **15**
Bramwell Av. CH43: Pren 6E **21**
Brancepeth Ct.
CH65: Ell P 4B **50**
Brancote Ct. CH43: C'ton 1C **20**
Brancote Gdns.
CH62: Brom 4B **36**
Brancote Mt. CH43: C'ton 1D **20**
Brancote Rd. CH43: C'ton 1D **20**
Brandon St. CH41: Birk 1B **22**
Bran St. L8: Liv 2G **23**
Brasenose Rd. L20: Boot 1D **6**
Brassey St. CH41: Birk 5E **13**
L8: Liv 1G **23**
Brattan Rd. CH41: Birk 3G **21**
Braunton Rd. CH45: Wall 5E **5**
Bray St. CH41: Birk 5F **13**
Breck, The CH66: Ell P 6E **43**
Breckfield Pl. L5: Liv 6H **7**
Breckfield Rd. Nth.
L5: Liv 5H **7**
Breck Pl. CH44: Wall 2E **13**
Breck Rd. CH44: Wall 1D **12**
L5: Liv 1H **15**
Breckside Av. CH44: Wall 1C **12**
Brecon Dr. CH66: Gt Sut 6E **49**
Brecon Rd. CH42: Tran 6G **21**
Bredon Cl. CH66: Lit Sut 1A **48**
Breeze Hill L9: Walt 1H **7**
L20: Boot 1F **7**
Breezehill Cl. CH64: Nest 5C **38**
Breezehill Pk. CH64: Nest 5D **38**
Breezehill Rd.
CH64: Nest 5D **38**
Brenig St. CH41: Birk 4D **12**
Brentwood Ct.
*CH49: W'chu 5G **19***
(off Childwall Grn.)
Brentwood St. CH44: Wall 2G **13**
Brereton Av. CH63: Beb 3G **29**
Brett St. CH41: Birk 5F **13**
Brewster St. L4: Boot 2G **7**
L20: Walt 2G **7**
Brian Av. CH61: Irby 3B **26**
Briardale Gdns.
CH66: Lit Sut 1C **48**
Briardale Rd. CH42: Tran 3G **21**
CH44: Wall 3A **14**
CH63: High B 2F **29**
CH64: Will 5C **40**
CH66: Lit Sut 1C **48**
Briar Dr. CH60: Hes 3C **32**
Briarfield Rd.
CH60: Hes 3D **32**
CH65: Ell P 2H **49**
Briar St. L4: Kirk 4F **7**
Briarswood Cl.
CH42: R Ferr 1F **29**
Briary Cl. CH60: Hes 2D **32**
Brick St. L1: Liv 6F **15**
Bride St. L4: Walt 1H **7**
Bridge Ct. CH48: W Kir 4C **16**
CH64: Nest 6C **38**
Bridgecroft Rd. CH45: Wall 5F **5**
Bridge Farm Cl.
CH49: W'chu 3H **19**
Bridge Mdw. CH66: Gt Sut 5F **49**
Bridgenorth Rd.
CH61: Pens 5A **26**
Bridge Rd. CH48: W Kir 4C **16**
Bridges Rd. CH65: Ell P 2D **50**
Bridge St. CH41: Birk 6A **14**
(not continuous)
CH62: Port S 4H **29**
(not continuous)
CH64: Nest 6C **38**
L20: Boot 1D **6**
Bridgewater St. L1: Liv 6F **15**
Bri. Wood Dr. CH66: Gt Sut . . .5C **48**
Bridle Av. CH44: Wall 3A **14**
Bridle Cl. CH43: Bid 1H **19**
CH62: Brom 4C **36**
Bridle Pk. CH62: Brom 4B **36**
Bridle Rd. CH44: Wall 3A **14**
CH62: Brom 4C **36**
Bridle Way CH66: Gt Sut 4D **48**
Bridport St. L3: Liv 3G **15**
Briedden Way
CH66: Lit Sut 1A **48**
Brighton St. CH44: Wall 1H **13**
Bright St. CH41: Birk 1G **21**
(not continuous)
L6: Liv 2H **15**
Bright Ter. L8: Liv 4H **23**
Brightwell Cl. CH49: Upton . . .3F **19**
Brill St. CH41: Birk 5F **13**
BRIMSTAGE **1B 34**
Brimstage Av.
CH63: High B 1D **28**
Brimstage Cl. CH60: Hes 4E **33**
Brimstage Grn.
CH60: Hes 3F **33**
Brimstage Hall **1A 34**
Brimstage La.
CH63: Brim, Store 5B **28**
Brimstage Rd. CH60: Hes 4E **33**
CH63: Beb, Brim, High B
. . . . .1C **34**
L4: Walt 1G **7**
Brimstage St. CH41: Birk 2G **21**
Brindley St. L8: Liv 1F **23**
Brinley Cl. CH62: Brom 6B **36**
Brisbane Av. CH45: New B 3E **5**
Briscoe Av. CH46: More 6E **11**
Briscoe Dr. CH46: More 6E **11**
Bristol Av. CH44: Wall 1G **13**
Bristol Dr. CH66: Gt Sut 6E **49**
Britannia Cres. L8: Liv 4H **23**
Britannia Pav. L3: Liv 5E **15**
Britannia Rd. CH45: Wall 6E **5**
Broadbelt St. L4: Walt 1H **7**
Broadfield Av. CH43: Bid 5H **11**
Broadfield Cl. CH43: Bid 6A **12**
Broadheath Av. CH43: Bid 6A **12**
Broadlake CH64: Will 5B **40**
Broadland Gdns.
CH66: Gt Sut 5F **49**
Broadland Rd.
CH66: Gt Sut 5F **49**
Broad La. CH60: Hes 2G **31**
Broadmead CH60: Hes 4E **33**
Broadoaks CH49: Upton 1E **19**
Broadstone Dr. CH63: Spit 1F **35**
Broadway CH45: Wall 6D **4**
CH49: Grea 2E **19**
CH63: High B 2D **28**
Broadway Av. CH45: Wall 6D **4**
Brockley Av. CH45: New B 2F **5**
Brockmoor Twr. L4: Kirk 3F **7**
Brock St. L4: Kirk 3G **7**
BROMBOROUGH **3A 36**
BROMBOROUGH POOL **4B 30**
BROMBOROUGH PORT **6C 30**
Bromborough Rake Station (Rail)
. . . .**3A 36**
Bromborough Rd.
CH63: Beb 4G **29**
Bromborough Station (Rail)
. . . .**4A 36**
Bromborough Village Rd.
CH62: Brom 2B **36**
Brome Way CH63: Spit 1H **35**
Bromley Cl. CH60: Hes 4A **32**
Bromley Rd. CH45: New B 4E **5**
Brompton Av. CH44: Wall 1G **13**
Brompton Way
CH66: Gt Sut 6E **49**
Bromsgrove Rd.
CH49: Grea 3C **18**
Bronington Av.
CH62: Brom 5B **36**
Bronte St. L3: Liv 3G **15**
Brook Cl. CH44: Wall 6G **5**
Brookdale Av. Nth.
CH49: Grea 3E **19**
Brookdale Av. Sth.
CH49: Grea 3E **19**
Brookdale Cl. CH49: Grea 3E **19**
Brookfield Gdns.
CH48: W Kir 5D **16**
Brookfield Rd.
CH48: W Kir 5D **16**
Brook Hey CH64: Park 3A **38**
BROOKHURST **6A 36**
Brookhurst Av. CH62: East 5A **36**
CH63: Brom, East 5A **36**
Brookhurst Cl.
CH63: Brom 6A **36**
Brookhurst Rd.
CH63: Brom 5A **36**
Brookland Rd. CH41: Birk 2H **21**
Brooklands CH41: Birk 6H **13**
Brooklands Gdns.
CH64: Park 4A **38**
Brooklands Rd. CH64: Park . . .4A **38**
Brook La. CH64: Park 3A **38**
Brooklet Rd. CH60: Hes 3E **33**
Brooklyn Dr. CH65: Gt Sut 2F **49**
Brook Mdw. CH61: Irby 2A **26**
Brook Rd. CH66: Gt Sut 2D **48**
Brooks All. L1: Liv 4F **15**
Brookside Cres.
CH49: Upton 2D **18**
Brookside Dr.
CH49: Upton 2E **19**
Brook St. CH41: Birk 5G **13**
CH62: Port S 3G **29**
CH64: Nest 5C **38**
L3: Liv 3D **14**
Brook St. E. CH41: Birk 6A **14**
Brook Ter. CH48: W Kir 5D **16**
Brookthorpe Cl. CH45: Wall 5F **5**
Brook Wlk. CH61: Irby 2H **25**
Brookway CH43: Pren 6C **20**
CH45: Wall 6E **5**
CH49: Grea 2E **19**
Brook Well CH64: Lit N 2C **44**
Broomfield Cl. CH60: Hes 2H **31**
Broom Hill CH43: C'ton 6D **12**
Broomlands CH60: Hes 3B **32**
Broomleigh Cl.
CH63: High B 4D **28**
Broseley Av. CH62: Brom 2A **36**
Broster Av. CH46: More 5C **10**
Broster Cl. CH46: More 5C **10**
Brosters La. CH47: Meols 4G **9**
Brotherton Cl.
CH62: Brom 2A **36**
Brotherton Rd.
CH44: Wall 3A **14**
Brougham Av. CH41: Tran 3B **22**
Brougham Rd.
CH44: Wall 2H **13**
Brougham Ter. L6: Liv 2H **15**
Broughton Av.
CH48: W Kir 4C **16**
Broughton Rd. CH44: Wall 2F **13**
Brow La. CH60: Hes 4B **32**
Browning Av.
CH42: R Ferr 6B **22**
Browning Dr.
CH65: Gt Sut 3F **49**
Browning Grn.
CH65: Gt Sut 3F **49**
Browning Rd. CH45: Wall 6B **4**
Brownlow Hill L3: Liv 4G **15**
Brownlow Rd.
CH62: New F 2H **29**
Brownlow St. L3: Liv 4H **15**
Brow Rd. CH43: Bid 4B **12**
Brow Side L5: Liv 1H **15**
Broxton Av. CH43: Pren 5D **20**
CH48: W Kir 4E **17**
Broxton Rd. CH45: Wall 5D **4**
CH66: Ell P 2E **49**
Bruce Cres. CH63: Brom 5A **36**
Bruce Dr. CH66: Gt Sut 3C **48**
Bruce St. L8: Liv 3H **23**
Bruera Rd. CH65: Gt Sut 3F **49**
Brunel M. L5: Liv 6H **7**
Brunel Rd. CH62: Brom 2D **36**
Brunsborough Cl.
CH62: Brom 5A **36**
Brunsfield Cl.
CH46: More 6C **10**
Brunstath Cl. CH60: Hes 2E **33**
Brunswick Bus. Pk.
L3: Liv 2F **23**
(not continuous)
Brunswick Cl. L4: Kirk 3G **7**
Brunswick Ct. CH41: Birk 6A **14**
Brunswick Cres.
CH66: Gt Sut 4E **49**
Brunswick Ent. Cen.
L3: Liv 2F **23**
Brunswick M. CH41: Birk 6A **14**
Brunswick Pl. L20: Kirk 3D **6**
Brunswick Rd. L6: Liv 2H **15**
Brunswick Station (Rail) **3G 23**
Brunswick St. L2: Liv 4E **15**
L3: Liv 4D **14**
Brunswick Way L3: Liv 2F **23**
Bryanston Rd. CH42: Tran 5E **21**
Bryn Bank CH44: Wall 1G **13**
Brynmoss Av. CH44: Wall 1D **12**
Bryony Way CH42: R Ferr 1F **29**
Brythen St. L1: Liv 4F **15**
Buccleuch St. CH41: Birk 4D **12**
Buchanan Rd. CH44: Wall 2H **13**
L9: Walt 1H **7**
Buckingham Av.
CH43: C'ton 6D **12**
CH63: High B 2E **29**
Buckingham Gdns.
CH65: Ell P 5B **50**
Buckingham Rd.
CH44: Wall 1D **12**
Buckingham St. L5: Liv 6G **7**
Buckland Dr. CH63: Spit 1F **35**
Buckley La. CH64: Will 5B **40**
Bude Cl. CH43: Bid 1A **20**
Budworth Cl. CH43: O'ton 3C **20**
Budworth Ct. CH43: O'ton 2D **20**
Budworth Rd.
CH43: Noct, O'ton 3C **20**
CH66: Gt Sut 5E **49**
Buerton Cl. CH43: Noct 3C **20**
Buffs La. CH60: Hes 2D **32**
Buggen La. CH64: Nest 5B **38**
Buildwas Rd. CH64: Nest 3C **38**
Bulkeley Rd. CH44: Wall 2H **13**
Bullens Rd. L4: Walt 3H **7**
Bull Hill CH64: Lit N 1D **44**
Bullrush Dr. CH46: More 3G **11**
Bulrushes, The L17: Aig 4H **23**
Bulwer St. CH42: R Ferr 5B **22**
Bunbury Grn. CH65: Ell P 5B **50**
Bungalows, The
*CH63: Thorn H 5B **34***
(off Raby Rd.)
Burbo Way CH45: Wall 3C **4**
Burden Rd. CH46: More 5C **10**
Burdett Av. CH63: Spit 1F **35**
Burdett Cl. CH63: Spit 1G **35**
Burdett Rd. CH45: Wall 6B **4**
CH66: Gt Sut 5E **49**
Burford Av. CH44: Wall 2D **12**
Burgess St. L3: Liv 3G **15**
Burleigh M. L5: Liv 4H **7**
Burleigh Rd. Nth. L5: Liv 4H **7**
Burleigh Rd. Sth. L5: Liv 5H **7**
Burlingham Av.
CH48: W Kir 6F **17**
Burlington Rd. CH45: New B . . .2F **5**
Burlington St. CH41: Birk 1A **22**
L3: Liv 1E **15**
Burnand St. L4: Walt 4H **7**
Burnell Rd. CH65: Ell P 3C **50**
Burnley Av. CH46: More 5F **11**
Burnley Cl. L6: Liv 1H **15**
Burnley Gro. CH46: More 4F **11**
Burnley Rd. CH46: More 4F **11**
Burns Av. CH45: Wall 6E **5**
Burns Cl. CH66: Gt Sut 3E **49**
Burnside Av. CH44: Wall 3F **13**
Burnside Rd. CH44: Wall 3F **13**
Burrell Cl. CH42: Tran 6G **21**
Burrell Ct. CH42: Tran 6G **21**
Burrell Dr. CH46: More 6D **10**
Burrell Rd. CH42: Tran 1B **28**
Burrell St. L4: Walt 3H **7**
Burroughs Gdns. L3: Liv 1F **15**
Burrows Ct. L3: Liv 6E **7**
BURTON **6H 45**
Burton Av. CH45: Wall 6C **4**
Burton Cl. L1: Liv 5F **15**
Burton Grn. CH66: Gt Sut 3D **48**
Burton Rd. CH64: Lit N 6C **38**
Burton St. L5: Kirk 5D **6**
Busby's Cotts. CH45: New B . . .3F **5**
Bushell Cl. CH64: Nest 6D **38**
Bushell Ct. CH43: O'ton 3E **21**
Bushell Rd. CH64: Nest 6D **38**
Bush Way CH60: Hes 3A **32**

Bute St.—Charlotte's Mdw.

Bute St. L5: Liv 1G **15**
(not continuous)
Buttercup Cl. CH46: More 3G **11**
Butterfield St. L4: Walt 4H **7**
Buttermere Av.
CH43: Noct 1A **20**
CH65: Ell P 4A **50**
Buttermere Ct. *CH41: Birk 2G 21*
(off Penrith St.)
Butterton Av. CH49: Upton 1D **18**
Button St. L2: Liv 4E **15**
Buxton La. CH44: Wall 6C **4**
Buxton Rd. CH42: R Ferr 5C **22**
Byerley St. CH44: Wall 3H **13**
Byles St. L8: Liv 3H **23**
Byng St. L20: Boot 1D **6**
Byrne Av. CH42: R Ferr 6B **22**
Byrne Avenue Recreation Cen.
6B **22**
Byrom St. L3: Liv 2F **15**
Byron Cl. CH43: Pren 1H **27**

C

Cablehouse *L2: Liv 3E 15*
(off Cheapside)
Cable Rd. CH47: Hoy 6D **8**
Cable St. L1: Liv 4E **15**
Cadmus Wlk. L6: Liv 1H **15**
Caernarvon Cl.
CH49: Upton 1G **19**
Caernarvon Ct. CH63: Beb 5F **29**
CH65: Ell P 5B **50**
Caerwys Gro. CH42: Tran 3A **22**
Cairo St. L4: Kirk 2G **7**
Caithness Dr. CH45: Wall 5G **5**
Caithness Gdns.
CH43: Pren 6D **20**
Calday Grange Cl.
CH48: W Kir 6F **17**
Caldbeck Rd. CH62: Brom 1B **36**
Calder Av. CH43: Pren 5D **20**
Calder Rd. CH63: High B 4D **28**
L5: Liv 5H **7**
Calder Way CH66: Gt Sut 2C **48**
Caldicott Av. CH62: Brom 4B **36**
Caldwell Dr. CH49: W'chu 5H **19**
CALDY 2B **24**
Caldy Chase Dr.
CH48: Caldy 2B **24**
Caldy Ct. CH48: W Kir 6D **16**
Caldy Dr. CH66: Gt Sut 3D **48**
Caldy Rd. CH45: Wall 6F **5**
CH48: Caldy, W Kir 6D **16**
Caldy Wood CH48: Caldy 2B **24**
Caledonia St. L7: Liv 5H **15**
Callaghan Cl. L5: Liv 6F **7**
Calmet Cl. L5: Liv 5G **7**
Calne Cl. CH61: Irby 2H **25**
Calthorpe Way CH43: Noct 1B **20**
Calveley Av. CH62: East 1H **41**
Calveley Cl. CH43: O'ton 4D **20**
Cambrian Cl. CH46: More 6C **10**
CH66: Lit Sut 1A **48**
Cambrian Rd.
CH46: More 6C **10**
Cambridge Ct.
CH65: Ell P 2A **50**
L7: Liv 4H **15**
(not continuous)
Cambridge Rd.
CH42: Tran 5F **21**
CH45: New B 4F **5**
CH62: Brom 3C **36**
CH65: Ell P 2A **50**
L20: Boot 1F **7**
Cambridge St. L7: Liv 5H **15**
(not continuous)
Camden Pl. CH41: Birk 1H **21**
Camden Rd. CH65: Ell P 2G **49**
Camden St. CH41: Birk 6A **14**
L3: Liv 3G **15**
Camelia Ct. L17: Aig 5H **23**
Cameron Rd. CH46: Leas 2H **11**
Cammell Ct. CH43: C'ton 1F **21**
Campbell Sq. *L1: Liv 5F 15*
(off Argyle St.)
Campbell St. L1: Liv 5F **15**
Campbeltown Rd.
CH41: Tran 2B **22**
Camperdown St.
CH41: Birk 1B **22**
Canada Blvd. L3: Liv 4D **14**
Canal Bri. Ent. Cen.
CH65: Ell P 1B **50**
Canalside CH65: Ell P 1B **50**
Canalside Gro. L5: Liv 6E **7**
Canalside Ind. Est.
CH65: Ell P 2H **43**
Canal St. L20: Boot 1D **6**
(not continuous)
Candia Towers
L5: Liv 5G **7**
Cannell Ct. CH64: Will 5C **40**
Canning Pl. L1: Liv 4E **15**
Canning St. CH41: Birk 6A **14**
L8: Liv 5H **15**
Cannon Hill CH43: C'ton 1F **21**
Cannon Mt. CH43: C'ton 1F **21**
Cannon St. CH65: Ell P 2G **49**
Canterbury Cl.
CH66: Gt Sut 6A **48**
Canterbury Rd.
CH42: R Ferr 6C **22**
CH44: Wall 2G **13**
Canterbury St. L3: Liv 2G **15**
Canterbury Way L3: Liv 2G **15**
Capenhurst Gdns.
CH66: Gt Sut 6D **48**
Capenhurst La. CH1: Cap 6C **48**
CH65: Whit 4F **49**
CH66: Gt Sut 6D **48**
Capenhurst Station (Rail)
6C **48**
Capital Ga. *L3: Liv 3H 15*
(off Daulby St.)
Carden Cl. L4: Kirk 4G **7**
Cardiff Cl. CH66: Gt Sut 6A **48**
Cardigan Av. CH41: Birk 1H **21**
Cardigan Rd. CH45: New B 4F **5**
Cardus Cl. CH46: More 5B **10**
Carey Av. CH63: High B 3D **28**
Cargill Gro. CH42: R Ferr 1H **29**
Carham Rd. CH47: Hoy 1E **17**
Carisbrooke Cl.
CH48: Caldy 1A **24**
Carisbrooke Pl.
L4: Kirk 2H **7**
Carisbrooke Rd.
L4: Kirk, Walt 1G **7**
L20: Boot 1G **7**
Carlaw Rd. CH42: Tran 5E **21**
Carlett Blvd. CH62: East 6D **36**
Carlett Pk. CH62: East 5D **36**
Carlisle Cl. CH43: O'ton 2G **21**
Carlisle M. CH43: O'ton 2G **21**
Carlton Cl. CH64: Park 3A **38**
Carlton Cres. CH66: Ell P 5F **43**
Carlton La. CH47: Meols 5E **9**
Carlton Mt. CH42: Tran 4A **22**
Carlton Rd. CH42: Tran 3G **21**
CH45: New B 3F **5**
CH63: Beb 5H **29**
Carlton St. L3: Liv 1D **14**
Carlton Ter. CH47: Meols 5E **9**
Carlyle Cres.
CH66: Gt Sut 3E **49**
Carmarthen Cres. L8: Liv 1F **23**
Carmel Cl. CH45: New B 3F **5**
Carmichael Av.
CH49: Grea 5D **18**
Carnarvon Ct. L9: Walt 1H **7**
Carnforth Cl. CH41: Birk 2G **21**
Carnoustie Cl.
CH46: More 4B **10**
Carnsdale Rd.
CH46: More 5F **11**
Carol Dr. CH60: Hes 3E **33**
Caroline Pl. CH43: O'ton 2F **21**
Carpenter's La.
CH48: W Kir 5D **16**
Carpenters Row L1: Liv 5E **15**
Carr Bri. Rd.
CH49: W'chu 3H **19**
Carr Ga. CH46: More 6B **10**
Carr Hey CH46: More 5B **10**
Carr Hey Cl. CH49: W'chu 5A **20**
Carr Ho. La.
CH46: More 5B **10**
Carrick Dr. CH65: Whit 5H **49**
Carrington Rd.
CH45: Wall 5F **5**
Carrington St. CH41: Birk 5E **13**
Carr La. CH46: More 4B **10**
CH47: Hoy 1D **16**
CH47: Meols 4A **10**
CH47: W Kir 2F **17**
CH48: W Kir 2F **17**
Carr La. Ind. Est.
CH47: Hoy 1E **17**
Carrock Rd. CH62: Brom 1C **36**
Carrow Cl. CH46: More 6B **10**
Carruthers St. L3: Liv 2E **15**
Carsgoe Rd. CH47: Hoy 1E **17**
Carsthorne Rd.
CH47: Hoy 1E **17**
Carters, The CH49: Grea 3C **18**
Carter St. L8: Liv 6H **15**
Carterton Rd. CH47: Hoy 1E **17**
Cartmel Cl. CH41: Birk 2G **21**
Cartmel Dr. CH46: More 6E **11**
CH66: Gt Sut 5F **49**
Carver St. L3: Liv 2H **15**
Caryl Gro. L8: Liv 3G **23**
Caryl St. L8: Liv 2G **23**
(Park St.)
L8: Liv 1F **23**
(Stanhope St.)
L8: Liv 2F **23**
(Warwick St.)
Cases St. L1: Liv 4F **15**
Cashel Rd. CH41: Birk 3F **13**
Cassio St. L20: Boot 1G **7**
Castle Cl. CH46: Leas 2G **11**
Castle Dr. CH60: Hes 3B **32**
CH65: Whit 4G **49**
Castlefields CH46: Leas 1F **11**
Castleford Ri. CH46: Leas 2E **11**
Castlegrange Cl.
CH46: Leas 1E **11**
Castleheath Cl.
CH46: Leas 2E **11**
Castle Hill *L2: Liv 4E 15*
(off Lwr. Castle St.)
Castle Mt. CH60: Hes 3B **32**
Castle Rd. CH45: Wall 5E **5**
Castle St. CH41: Birk 1B **22**
L2: Liv 4E **15**
Castleway Nth.
CH46: Leas 1G **11**
Castleway Sth.
CH46: Leas 2G **11**
Catharine St. L8: Liv 6H **15**
Cathcart St. CH41: Birk 6H **13**
Cathedral Cl. L1: Liv 6G **15**
Cathedral Ct. *L8: Liv 5H 15*
(off Gambier Ter.)
Cathedral Ga. L1: Liv 5G **15**
Cathedral Wlk. L3: Liv 4G **15**
Catherine St. CH41: Birk 1H **21**
Caulfield Dr. CH49: Grea 4E **19**
Causeway, The
CH62: Port S 4H **29**
(not continuous)
Causeway Cl.
CH62: Port S 3H **29**
Causeway Ho. CH46: Leas 1E **11**
Cavell Dr. CH65: Whit 3G **49**
Cavendish Dr.
CH42: R Ferr 6H **21**
Cavendish Gdns.
CH65: Whit 3G **49**
Cavendish Rd. CH41: Birk 6F **13**
CH45: New B 2F **5**
Cavendish St. CH41: Birk 5F **13**
Cavern Club, The *4E 15*
(off Mathew St.)
Cavern Quarter *4E 15*
(off Mathew St.)
Cavern Walks *L2: Liv 4E 15*
(off Mathew St.)
Cawood Cl. CH66: Lit Sut 2B **48**
Caxton Cl. CH43: Bid 1A **20**
CH66: Gt Sut 3F **49**
Cazneau St. L3: Liv 1F **15**
Cearns Rd. CH43: O'ton 2E **21**
Cecil Rd. CH42: Tran 5F **21**
CH45: Wall 1E **13**
CH62: New F 1H **29**
Cedab Rd. CH65: Ell P 1A **50**
Cedar Av. CH63: High B 5E **29**
CH66: Lit Sut 1C **48**
Cedardale Dr. CH66: Whit 6A **48**
Cedar Gro. CH64: Nest 5D **38**
Cedars, The CH46: More 6C **10**
Cedar St. CH41: Birk 2H **21**
Cedarway CH60: Hes 6D **32**
Cedarwood Cl.
CH49: Grea 3B **18**
Celia St. L20: Kirk 2F **7**
Celtic Rd. CH47: Meols 4G **9**
Celtic St. L8: Liv 1H **23**
Cemeas Cl. L5: Liv 6E **7**
Central Av. CH62: Brom 2A **36**
CH65: Ell P 3A **50**
Central Library *3F 15*
(off Cuerden St.)
Central Pk. Av.
CH44: Wall 1G **13**
Central Rd. CH62: Port S 2H **29**
(Primrose Hill)
CH62: Port S 4H **29**
(Wood St.)
Central Shop. Cen.
L1: Liv 4F **15**
Central Station (Rail) **4F 15**
Centurion Cl. CH47: Meols 4G **9**
Centurion Dr. CH47: Meols 4G **9**
Century Bldgs. L3: Liv 3F **23**
Ceres Ct. CH43: Bid 6A **12**
Ceres St. L20: Kirk 2E **7**
Cestrian Dr. CH61: Thing 4C **26**
Chadwick Ct. Ind. Cen.
L3: Liv 1D **14**
Chadwick St. CH46: More 5E **11**
L3: Liv 1D **14**
Chalfield Av.
CH66: Gt Sut 2C **48**
Chalfield Cl. CH66: Gt Sut 2C **48**
Chalkwell Dr. CH60: Hes 4E **33**
Challis St. CH41: Birk 4C **12**
Chaloner St. L3: Liv 6F **15**
Chamberlain St.
CH41: Tran 3A **22**
CH44: Wall 3E **13**
Chancel St. L4: Kirk 4F **7**
Change La. CH64: Will 5D **40**
Channel, The CH45: Wall 4C **4**
Chantrell Rd.
CH48: W Kir 5G **17**
Chantry Cl. CH43: Bid 1A **20**
Chantry Wlk. CH60: Hes 5C **32**
Chapel Cl. CH65: Ell P 2G **43**
Chapel Gdns. L5: Liv 6F **7**
Chapelhill Rd.
CH46: More 5F **11**
Chapel La.
CH1: Cap, W'bnk 6G **47**
CH66: Led 6G **47**
Chapel M. CH65: Whit 3H **49**
Chapel Rd. CH47: Hoy 5E **9**
Chapel St. L3: Liv 3D **14**
Chapel Ter. L20: Boot 1D **6**
Chapel Vw. CH62: East 5E **37**
Chapel Walks *L3: Liv 3D 14*
(off Chapel St.)
Chapman Cl. L8: Liv 2G **23**
Chapterhouse Cl.
CH65: Ell P 2C **50**
Charing Cross CH41: Birk 1G **21**
Charlcombe St. CH42: Tran 3H **21**
Charlecote St. L8: Liv 4H **23**
Charles Price Gdns.
CH65: Ell P 1A **50**
Charles Rd. CH47: Hoy 1D **16**
Charles St. CH41: Birk 6H **13**
Charleston Cl.
CH66: Gt Sut 4D **48**
Charleston Rd. L8: Liv 3G **23**
Charlesville CH43: O'ton 2F **21**
Charlesville Ct.
CH43: O'ton 2F **21**
Charlotte Rd. CH44: Wall 6G **5**
Charlotte's Mdw.
CH63: Beb 5G **29**

Charlotte Way—Collingham Grn.

Charlotte Way *L1: Liv* . . . .*4F* ***15*** *(off St Johns Cen.)*
Charlton Ct. CH43: C'ton 1D **20**
Charlwood Cl. CH43: Bid 1A **20**
Charter Cres.
CH66: Gt Sut 4E **49**
Charter Ho. CH44: Wall 1H **13**
Chase, The CH60: Hes 3C **32**
CH63: Brom 6A **36**
Chase Dr. CH66: Gt Sut 5E **49**
Chase Way CH66: Gt Sut 5E **49**
L5: Liv 1G **15**
Chatham Rd.
CH42: R Ferr 5C **22**
Chatham St. L7: Liv 5H **15**
Chatsworth Av.
CH44: Wall 1G **13**
Chatsworth Cl.
CH66: Gt Sut 2D **48**
Chatsworth Rd.
CH42: R Ferr 5C **22**
CH61: Pens 4B **26**
Chaucer St. L3: Liv 2F **15**
Cheapside L2: Liv 3E **15**
Cheapside All. *L2: Liv* . . . .*3E* ***15*** *(off Cheapside)*
Cheddon Way CH61: Pens 5A **26**
Chelford Cl. CH43: Bid 6A **12**
Chelmsford Cl. L4: Kirk 4F **7**
Cheltenham Cres.
CH46: Leas 2E **11**
Cheltenham Rd. CH45: Wall . . .5C **4**
CH65: Ell P 4B **50**
Chenotrie Gdns.
CH43: Noct 2B **20**
Chepstow Av. CH44: Wall 1G **13**
Chepstow St. L4: Walt 2G **7**
Cheriton Av. CH48: W Kir 5F **17**
Cherrybank CH44: Wall 3F **13**
Cherry Brow Ter.
CH64: Will . . . .*5B* ***40*** *(off Hadlow Rd.)*
Cherry Cl. CH64: Nest 5G **39**
Cherry Gdns. CH47: Hoy 6D **8**
Cherry Gro. CH66: Whit 6G **49**
Cherry Sq. CH44: Wall 1F **13**
Cherry Tree M. CH60: Hes 3C **32**
Cherry Tree Rd.
CH46: More 6F **11**
Chesham Ct. CH65: Ell P 3B **50**
Cheshire Acre
CH49: W'chu 5G **19**
Cheshire Gro.
CH46: More 6E **11**
Cheshire Oaks Bus. Pk.
CH65: Ell P 6B **50**
Cheshire Oaks Outlet Village
CH65: Ell P 5C **50**
Cheshire Oaks Way
CH65: Ell P 5C **50**
Cheshire Way CH61: Pens 6B **26**
Chesney Cl. L8: Liv 1G **23**
Chester Ct. CH63: Beb 5F **29**
Chesterfield Rd.
CH62: East 1F **41**
Chesterfield St. L8: Liv 6G **15**
Chester High Rd.
CH64: Burt, Nest, Will 6F **33**
Chester Rd. CH60: Hes 4D **32**
CH64: Nest 6C **38**
CH65: Whit 6B **48**
CH66: Chil T, Gt Sut,
Hoot, Lit Sut 4A **42**
CH66: Whit 6B **48**
Chester St. CH41: Birk 2B **22**
CH44: Wall 2E **13**
L8: Liv 6G **15**
Chestnut Av. CH66: Gt Sut 6F **49**
Chestnut Cl. CH49: Grea 6C **18**
Chestnut Gro.
CH42: Tran 3H **21**
CH62: Brom 3A **36**
Cheswood Ct.
CH49: W'chu . . . .*6G* ***19*** *(off Childwall Grn.)*
Chetwynd Cl. CH43: O'ton 3D **20**
Chetwynd Rd. CH43: O'ton . . .2E **21**
Cheverton Cl.
CH49: W'chu 4H **19**
Cheviot Cl. CH42: Tran 6H **21**
CH66: Lit Sut 1A **48**
Cheviot Rd. CH42: Tran 6G **21**
Chidden Cl. CH49: Grea 4C **18**
Childer Cres.
CH66: Lit Sut 6B **42**
Childer Gdns.
CH66: Lit Sut 6B **42**
CHILDER THORNTON **5A 42**
Childwall Av. CH46: More 6D **10**
Childwall Cl. CH46: More 6D **10**
Childwall Ct. CH66: Ell P 5F **43**
Childwall Gdns.
CH66: Ell P 5F **43**
Childwall Grn.
CH49: W'chu 5G **19**
Childwall Rd. CH66: Ell P 5F **43**
Chilhem Cl. L8: Liv 3H **23**
Chillingham St. L8: Liv 3H **23**
Chiltern Rd. CH42: Tran 6G **21**
Chilton Dr. CH66: Gt Sut 5E **49**
China Farm La.
CH48: W Kir 3G **17**
Chippenham Av.
CH49: Grea 3C **18**
Chirkdale St. L4: Kirk 2G **7**
Chirk Gdns. CH65: Ell P 4B **50**
Chirk Way CH46: More 6F **11**
Chisenhale St. L3: Liv 1E **15**
Cholmondeley Rd.
CH48: W Kir 5D **16**
CH65: Gt Sut 3F **49**
Cholsey Cl. CH49: Upton 3F **19**
Chorley Way CH63: Spit 2G **35**
Chorlton Gro. CH45: Wall 6B **4**
Christchurch Rd.
CH43: O'ton 3F **21**
Christian St. L3: Liv 2F **15**
Christie Cl. CH66: Hoot 3A **42**
Christleton Cl.
CH43: O'ton 5B **20**
Christleton Dr. CH66: Ell P . . .1E **49**
Christmas St. L20: Kirk 2F **7**
Christopher Dr. CH62: East . . .6E **37**
Christophers Cl.
CH61: Pens 5C **26**
Christopher St. L4: Walt 3H **7**
Chung Hok Ho. *L1: Liv* . . . . . .*6G* ***15*** *(off Pine M.)*
Church All. L1: Liv 4F **15**
Church Cl. CH44: Wall 1H **13**
Church Ct. CH49: Upton 1E **19**
Church Cres. CH44: Wall 3A **14**
Church Dr. CH62: Port S 3H **29**
Church Farm Ct.
CH60: Hes 4B **32**
CH64: Will 5B **40**
Church Flats L4: Walt 1H **7**
Church Gdns. CH44: Wall 1H **13**
Church Hill CH45: Wall 6D **4**
Churchill Av. CH41: Birk 6F **13**
Churchill Ct. CH64: Nest 5C **38**
Churchill Gro. CH44: Wall 6G **5**
Churchill Way CH64: Nest 5C **38**
Churchill Way Nth. L3: Liv 3F **15**
Churchill Way Sth. L3: Liv 3F **15**
Churchlands *CH44: Wall* . . . . .*3A* ***14*** *(off Bridle Rd.)*
Church La. CH44: Wall . . . . . .1H **13** (not continuous)
CH49: W'chu 5H **19**
CH61: Thurs 4F **25**
CH62: Brom 2B **36**
CH62: East 6E **37**
CH64: Nest 6C **38**
CH66: Gt Sut 3D **48**
L4: Walt 1H **7**
Churchmeadow Cl.
CH44: Wall 1H **13**
Church Mdw. La.
CH60: Hes 4A **32**
Church M. CH42: R Ferr 6C **22**
Church Pde. CH65: Ell P 1A **50**
Church Pl. CH42: Tran 4H **21**
Church Rd. CH42: Tran 4H **21**
CH44: Wall 3A **14**
CH48: W Kir 6C **16**
CH49: Upton 2G **19**
CH63: Beb 6G **29**
Church Rd. CH63: Thorn H . . .5B **34**
L4: Walt 1H **7**
Church Rd. W. L4: Walt 1H **7**
Church Sq. CH62: Brom 2B **36**
Church St. CH41: Birk . . . . . . .1B **22** (not continuous)
CH44: Wall 1H **13**
CH65: Ell P 1A **50**
L1: Liv 4F **15**
L20: Boot 1C **6**
Church Ter. CH42: Tran 4H **21**
Churchview Rd.
CH41: Birk 5F **13**
Church Wlk. CH48: W Kir 6D **16**
CH65: Ell P 1A **50**
L20: Boot 1D **6**
Churchwood Cl.
CH62: Brom 2B **36**
Churchwood Ct.
CH49: W'chu 6H **19**
Churnet St. L4: Kirk 3G **7**
Churn Way CH49: Grea 3D **18**
Churton Av. CH43: O'ton 4D **20**
Churton Ct. L6: Liv 2H **15**
Circular Dr. CH49: Grea 4D **18**
CH60: Hes 2B **32**
CH62: Port S 2H **29**
Circular Rd. CH41: Birk 2H **21**
Cirencester Av.
CH49: Grea 3C **18**
Citrine Rd. CH44: Wall 3H **13**
City Rd. L4: Walt 2H **7**
Civic Way CH63: Beb 4G **29**
CH65: Ell P 3H **49**
CLAIRE HOUSE CHILDREN'S HOSPICE **2D 34**
Clare Cres. CH44: Wall 6D **4**
Clare Dr. CH65: Whit 5H **49**
Claremont Ct. CH45: Wall 5D **4**
Claremont Rd.
CH48: W Kir 4D **16**
Claremont Way
CH63: High B 1D **28**
Claremount Dr. CH63: Beb 5F **29**
Claremount Rd.
CH45: Wall 4D **4**
Clarence Rd. CH42: Tran 4G **21**
CH44: Wall 3H **13**
Clarence St. L3: Liv 4G **15**
Clarendon Cl.
CH43: O'ton 2G **21**
Clarendon Rd.
CH44: Wall 2H **13**
Clare Rd. L20: Boot 1F **7**
Clare Way CH45: Wall 6D **4**
Claribel St. L8: Liv 1H **23**
Clarke Av. CH42: R Ferr 5A **22**
CLATTERBRIDGE HOSPITAL **2D 34**
Clatterbridge Rd.
CH63: Spit 3D **34**
CLAUGHTON **6D 12**
Claughton Dr. CH44: Wall 2F **13**
Claughton Firs
CH43: O'ton 3F **21**
Claughton Grn.
CH43: O'ton 2E **21**
Claughton Pl. CH41: Birk 1G **21**
Claughton Rd. CH41: Birk 1G **21**
Clayfield Cl. L20: Boot 1F **7**
Clayhill Grn.
CH66: Lit Sut 6C **42**
Clayhill Ind. Est.
CH64: Nest 3C **38**
Clayhill Light Ind. Pk.
CH64: Nest 3D **38**
Clay St. L3: Liv 1D **14**
Clayton La. CH44: Wall 3E **13**
Clayton Pl. CH41: Birk 2G **21**
Clayton Sq. L1: Liv 4F **15**
Clayton Sq. Shop. Cen.
L1: Liv . . . .*4F* ***15*** *(off Clayton Sq.)*
Clayton St. CH41: Birk 2G **21**
Clee Hill Rd. CH42: Tran 6G **21**
Clegg St. L5: Liv 1G **15**
Clement Gdns. L3: Liv 1E **15**
Cleopas St. L8: Liv 3H **23**
Cleveland Bldgs. L1: Liv 5E **15**
Cleveland Dr.
CH66: Lit Sut 1A **48**
Cleveland Sq. L1: Liv 5F **15**
Cleveland St. CH41: Birk 5F **13**
Cleveley Rd. CH47: Meols 5G **9**
Cliff, The CH45: New B 2D **4**
Cliff Dr. CH44: Wall 6H **5**
Cliffe Rd. CH64: Lit N 2D **44**
Clifford Rd. CH44: Wall 2F **13**
Clifford St. CH41: Birk 5E **13**
L3: Liv 3G **15**
Cliff Rd. CH44: Wall 2D **12**
Clifton Av. CH62: East 2G **41**
Clifton Ct. CH41: Birk 2H **21**
Clifton Cres. CH41: Birk 1A **22**
Clifton Gdns. CH65: Ell P 4A **50**
Clifton Ga. CH41: Birk 2H **21**
Clifton Gro. CH44: Wall 1G **13**
L5: Liv 1G **15**
CLIFTON PARK **2H 21**
Clifton Rd. CH41: Birk 2H **21**
Clifton Vs. CH1: Back 6B **48**
Clipper Vw. CH62: New F 1H **29**
Clive Rd. CH43: O'ton 3F **21**
Cloister Way CH65: Ell P 2C **50**
Close, The CH49: Grea 5D **18**
CH61: Irby 3H **25**
CH63: High B 6H **21**
Closeburn Av. CH60: Hes 5A **32**
Clover Dr. CH41: Birk 4C **12**
Cloverfield Gdns.
CH66: Lit Sut 6D **42**
Clwyd St. CH41: Birk 1H **21**
CH45: New B 4E **5**
Clwyd Way CH66: Lit Sut 1A **48**
Clydesdale CH65: Whit 4H **49**
Clydesdale Rd. CH44: Wall 6H **5**
CH47: Hoy 5D **8**
Clyde St. CH42: R Ferr 5B **22**
L20: Kirk 3E **7**
Coalbrookdale Rd.
CH64: Nest 3C **38**
Coal St. L1: Liv 3G **15**
Coastal Dr. CH45: Wall 3B **4**
Coastguard La.
CH64: Park 4A **38**
Cobden Av. CH42: Tran 4B **22**
Cobden Ct. CH42: Tran 4A **22**
Cobden Pl. CH42: Tran 4B **22**
Cobden St. L6: Liv 2H **15**
Cobham Rd. CH46: More 6D **10**
Coburg St. CH41: Birk 1H **21**
Coburg Wharf L3: Liv 1E **23**
Cochrane St. L5: Liv 6H **7**
Cockburn St. L8: Liv 3H **23**
Cockerell Cl. L4: Walt 4H **7**
Cockspur St. L3: Liv 3E **15**
Cockspur St. W.
L3: Liv 3E **15**
Cokers, The CH42: High B 1E **29**
Coldstream Dr.
CH66: Lit Sut 2H **47**
Coleman Dr. CH49: Grea 4C **18**
Colemere Ct. CH65: Ell P 6H **43**
Colemere Dr.
CH61: Thing 3D **26**
Coleridge Dr.
CH62: New F 2G **29**
Cole St. CH43: O'ton 1G **21**
Colin Dr. L3: Liv 6E **7**
Coliseum Shop. & Leisure Pk.
CH65: Ell P 5B **50**
Coliseum Way
CH65: Ell P 6B **50**
College Cl. CH43: Bid 1H **19**
CH45: Wall 5C **4**
College Dr. CH63: Beb 2G **29**
College La. L1: Liv 4F **15**
College St. Nth. L6: Liv 2H **15**
College St. Sth. L6: Liv 2H **15**
College Vw. L20: Boot 1E **7**
Colliery Grn. Cl.
CH64: Lit N 2C **44**
Colliery Grn. Ct.
CH64: Lit N 2C **44**
Colliery Grn. Dr.
CH64: Lit N 2C **44**
Collingham Grn.
CH66: Lit Sut 2B **48**

Collingwood Rd.
  CH63: Beb 5H 29
Collin Rd. CH43: Bid 5C 12
Colmore Av. CH63: Spit 2F 35
Colonnades, The L3: Liv ...5D 14
Colquitt St. L1: Liv 5G 15
Columbia La. CH43: O'ton ..3F 21
Columbia Rd. CH43: O'ton ..3F 21
  L4: Walt 1H 7
Columbus Dr. CH61: Pens ..6A 26
Columbus Quay L3: Liv 4G 23
Column Rd.
  CH48: Caldy, W Kir 5E 17
Colville Rd. CH44: Wall 1E 13
Colwyn Cl. CH65: Ell P 4B 50
Colwyn St. CH41: Birk 5E 13
Combermere St. L8: Liv ...1G 23
Comely Av. CH44: Wall 1G 13
Comely Bank Rd.
  CH44: Wall 1H 13
Commercial Rd.
  CH62: Brom 6C 30
  L5: Kirk 5E 7
Common Fld. Rd.
  CH49: W'chu 6H 19
Commonwealth Pav.
  L3: Liv 5E 15
Commutation Row L1: Liv ..3F 15
Compass Ct. CH45: Wall 3D 4
Compton Pl. CH65: Ell P ...2H 49
Compton Rd. CH41: Birk ...4B 12
Comus St. L3: Liv 2F 15
Concert Sq. *L1: Liv* *4F 15*
  (off Concert St.)
Concert St. L1: Liv 4F 15
Concordia Av.
  CH49: Upton 2G 19
Concourse, The
  CH48: W Kir 4C 16
Coney Wlk. CH49: Upton ...1D 18
Conifer Cl. CH66: Whit 6B 48
Coningsby Dr. CH45: Wall ..1E 13
Coningsby Rd. L4: Walt 4H 7
  CH65: Ell P 4B 50
Coniston Av. CH43: Noct ...2A 20
  CH45: Wall 4C 4
  CH63: East 1E 41
Coniston Cl. CH66: Hoot ...4B 42
Coniston Dr. CH61: Irby ...3H 25
  CH64: Nest 1C 44
Connaught Cl. CH41: Birk ..5E 13
Connaught Way
  CH41: Birk 5D 12
Connolly Ho. L20: Boot 1E 7
Conservation Cen. *3F 15*
Constance St. L3: Liv 3H 15
Constantine Av.
  CH60: Hes 2C 32
Convent Cl. CH42: Tran 3H 21
Conville Blvd.
  CH63: High B 1D 28
Conway Cl. CH63: High B ..4D 28
Conway Ct. CH43: Beb 5F 29
  CH65: Ell P 4B 50
Conway Dr. CH41: Birk 1H 21
Conway Park Station (Rail)
  ....6A 14
Conway St. CH41: Birk 6G 13
  (not continuous)
  L5: Liv 6G 7
Cookes Cl. CH64: Nest 4C 38
Cookson St. L1: Liv 6G 15
Cook St. CH41: Birk 2G 21
  CH65: Ell P 1A 50
  L2: Liv 4E 15
Coombe Pk. CH66: Lit Sut ..1C 48
Coombe Pk. Ct.
  CH66: Lit Sut 1C 48
Coombe Rd. CH61: Irby 2A 26
Cooperage Cl. L8: Liv 3G 23
Copperas Hill L3: Liv 4G 15
Copperfield Cl. L8: Liv 2H 23
Coppice, The CH45: Wall ...4E 5
Coppice Cl. CH43: Bid 1H 19
Coppice Grange
  CH46: More 6C 10
Coppice Gro. CH49: Grea ..5C 18
Copse Gro. CH61: Irby 2A 26

Copsmead CH46: More 5F 11
Coral Ridge CH43: Bid 1B 20
Corbyn St. CH44: Wall 3A 14
Corfu St. CH41: Birk 1G 21
Corinthian St.
  CH42: R Ferr 5B 22
Corinth Twr. L5: Liv 5G 7
Corinto St. L8: Liv 6G 15
Cormorant Cl. CH44: Wall ..3C 4
Cornelius Dr. CH61: Pens ..4B 26
Cornfield Cl. CH66: Gt Sut ..6F 49
Cornflower Way
  CH46: More 3G 11
Cornhill L1: Liv 5E 15
Corniche Rd. CH62: Port S ..3H 29
Corn St. L8: Liv 2G 23
Cornwall Cl. CH62: New F ..1H 29
Cornwall Dr. CH63: Beb 5F 29
Cornwall Dr. CH43: Pren ...6E 21
Cornwallis St. L1: Liv 5F 15
  (not continuous)
Corona Rd. CH62: Port S ..3A 30
Coronation Av.
  CH45: New B 4F 5
Coronation Bldgs.
  CH45: Wall 1E 13
  CH48: W Kir 3E 17
Coronation Dr.
  CH62: Brom 6B 30
Coronation Rd.
  CH47: Hoy 1B 16
  CH65: Ell P 3H 49
  (not continuous)
Corporation Rd.
  CH41: Birk 5D 12
Corrie Dr. CH63: Beb 5F 29
Cortsway CH49: Grea 2E 19
Cortsway W. CH49: Grea ...2D 18
Corwen Cl. CH43: Bid 1H 19
  CH46: More 6F 11
Corwen Rd. CH47: Hoy 6E 9
Costain St. L20: Kirk 3E 7
Cotswold Rd. CH42: Tran ...6G 21
Cottage Cl. CH63: Brom ...6A 36
  CH64: Lit N 6C 38
Cottage Dr. E. CH60: Hes ..6B 32
Cottage Dr. W. CH60: Hes ..6B 32
Cottage La. CH60: Hes 6B 32
Cottage St. CH41: Birk 6H 13
Cottesmore Dr.
  CH60: Hes 3F 33
Cotton St. L3: Liv 1D 14
Coulsdon Pl. L8: Liv 3H 23
Coulthard Rd.
  CH42: R Ferr 1G 29
County Rd. L4: Walt 2H 7
County Sessions House *3F 15*
  (off Mill La.)
Court, The CH63: Beb 5G 29
  CH64: Lit N 1D 44
Court Av. CH47: Hoy 6C 8
Court Ho., The
  CH65: Ell P 1A 50
Courtenay Av. CH44: Wall ..2E 13
Courtney Rd.
  CH42: R Ferr 1G 29
Courtyard, The CH64: Will ..5B 40
Covent Gdn. L2: Liv 3D 14
Coventry Av. CH66: Gt Sut ..6A 48
Coventry Cl. CH41: Birk 1H 21
Covertside CH48: W Kir 5F 17
Cowan Dr. L6: Liv 1H 15
Coward Av. CH43: Bid 4A 12
Cow La. CH66: Lit Sut 1C 48
Cowley Cl. CH49: Upton ...2D 18
Cowley Rd. L4: Walt 2H 7
Craig Gdns. CH66: Ell P ...6E 43
Craigleigh Gro.
  CH62: East 1H 41
Cranborne Av.
  CH47: Meols 4G 9
Cranbourne Av.
  CH41: Birk 6E 13
  CH46: More 6D 10
Cranford Cl. CH62: East ...1H 41
Cranford St. CH44: Wall 3G 13
Cranmer St. L5: Liv 6E 7
  (not continuous)

Cranswick Grn.
  CH66: Lit Sut 2C 48
Cranwell Rd. CH49: Grea ...4B 18
Craven Cl. CH41: Birk 1H 21
Craven St. CH41: Birk 1G 21
  L3: Liv 3G 15
Creek, The CH45: Wall 3C 4
Creer St. L5: Liv 1G 15
Crescent, The
  CH48: W Kir 5C 16
  CH49: Grea 4D 18
  CH60: Hes 5D 32
  CH61: Pens 3B 26
  CH63: High B 4E 29
  CH65: Gt Sut 2F 49
Crescent Rd. CH44: Wall ...1G 13
  CH65: Ell P 1B 50
Cressida Av. CH63: High B ..2E 29
Cressingham Rd.
  CH45: New B 3F 5
Cressington Av.
  CH42: Tran 6H 21
Cressington Gdns.
  CH65: Ell P 1A 50
Cresson Ct. CH43: O'ton ...2D 20
Cresswell St. L6: Liv 1H 15
  (not continuous)
Crete Towers L5: Liv 5G 7
Crewe Grn. CH49: W'chu ...5G 19
Criccieth Ct. CH65: Ell P ...5B 50
Criftin Cl. CH66: Gt Sut 5C 48
Crocus Av. CH41: Birk 5D 12
Crocus St. L5: Kirk 4F 7
Croesmere Dr.
  CH66: Gt Sut 5D 48
Croft, The CH49: Grea 5D 18
Croft Av. CH62: Brom 2A 36
Croft Av. E. CH62: Brom ...1B 36
Croft Bus. Cen.
  CH62: Brom 1C 36
Croft Bus. Pk. CH62: Brom ..1B 36
Croft Cl. CH43: Noct 3C 20
Croft Cotts. *CH66: Chil T* ...*5A 42*
  (off School La.)
Croft Ct. CH65: Ell P 4C 50
Croft Dr. CH46: More 6F 11
  CH48: Caldy 2A 24
Croft Dr. E. CH48: Caldy ...2B 24
Croft Dr. W. CH48: Caldy ..2A 24
Croft Edge CH43: O'ton 4F 21
Croften Dr. CH64: Lit N 2C 44
Crofters, The CH49: Grea ..3D 18
Crofters Cl. CH66: Gt Sut ..6E 49
Crofters Heath
  CH66: Gt Sut 6E 49
Croft Grn. CH62: Brom 6B 30
Croft La. CH62: Brom 2B 36
Crofton Rd. CH42: Tran 4A 22
Croft Technology Pk.
  CH62: Brom 2C 36
Croft Trade Pk.
  CH62: Brom 1C 36
Cromarty Rd. CH44: Wall ..1D 12
Cromer Dr. CH45: Wall 6E 5
Cromer Rd. CH47: Hoy 6C 8
Crompton St. L5: Liv 6F 7
Cromwell Rd. CH65: Ell P ..2A 50
  L4: Walt 1G 7
Cronton Av. CH46: Leas 2F 11
Croome Dr. CH48: W Kir ...5E 17
Cropper St. L1: Liv 4F 15
Crosby Cl. CH49: Upton ...1F 19
Crosby Gro. CH64: Will 4D 40
Crosfield Rd. CH44: Wall ...2G 13
Cross, The CH62: Brom 2C 36
  CH64: Nest 6C 38
Crossdale Rd.
  CH62: Brom 5B 36
Crosshall St. L1: Liv 4E 15
Cross Hey Av. CH43: Noct ..2B 20
Cross La. CH45: Wall 6B 4
  CH63: Beb 5F 29
  CH64: Lit N 2C 44
Crossley Av. CH66: Ell P ...1E 49
Crossley Dr. CH60: Hes 3H 31
Cross St. CH41: Birk 1B 22
  CH62: Port S 4H 29
  CH64: Nest 5C 38
Crossway CH43: Bid 5C 12

Crossway, The
  CH63: Raby 1G 39
Crossways CH62: Brom 6B 30
Crosthwaite Av.
  CH62: East 1H 41
Croughton Ct. CH66: Ell P ..5F 43
Croughton Rd. CH66: Ell P ..5F 43
Crowmarsh Cl.
  CH49: Upton 3F 19
Crown St. L7: Liv 3H 15
  (not continuous)
Crow St. L8: Liv 1F 23
Croxteth Av. CH44: Wall ...1F 13
Croylands St. L4: Kirk 3G 7
Crump St. L1: Liv 6G 15
Crutchley Av. CH41: Birk ...5F 13
Cubbin Cres. L5: Kirk 5F 7
Cuckoo La.
  CH64: Lit N, Nest 1F 45
Cuerden St. L3: Liv 3F 15
Cullen Cl. CH63: East 1E 41
Cumberland Av.
  CH43: Pren 5E 21
Cumberland Gro.
  CH66: Gt Sut 4C 48
Cumberland Rd.
  CH45: New B 4G 5
Cumberland St. L1: Liv 3E 15
Cumbers Dr. CH64: Ness ...2E 45
Cumbers La. CH64: Ness ...2E 45
Cumbrae Dr. CH65: Ell P ...6A 50
Cumbria Cl. CH66: Gt Sut ..6E 49
Cummings St. L1: Liv 5G 15
Cunard Av. CH44: Wall 6H 5
Cunard Cl. CH43: Bid 1A 20
Cunliffe St. L2: Liv 3E 15
Cunningham Cl.
  CH48: Caldy 3A 24
Cunningham Dr.
  CH63: Brom 3A 36
Curlender Cl. CH41: Birk ...4C 12
Curlew Cl. CH49: Upton ...1D 18
Curlew Ct. CH49: Upton ...1D 18
Curlew Ct. CH46: More 4C 10
Curlew Way CH46: More 4C 10
Curwell Cl. CH63: Spit 6H 29
Curzon Av. CH41: Birk 6F 13
  CH45: New B 3F 5
Curzon Rd. CH42: Tran 5F 21
  CH47: Hoy 6C 8
Custom Ho. La. L1: Liv 4E 15
Cygnet Cl. CH66: Gt Sut ...3D 48
Cypress Av. CH66: Gt Sut ..6F 49
Cypress Cft. CH63: Spit 6H 29
Cyprus Ter. CH45: New B ..4F 5

DACRE HILL 1F 29
Dacre St. CH41: Birk 1A 22
  L20: Boot 2D 6
Dacy Rd. L5: Liv 5H 7
Daffodil Rd. CH41: Birk 6D 12
Daisy St. L5: Kirk 4F 7
Dale, The CH64: Nest 1B 44
Dale Av. CH60: Hes 2B 32
  CH66: Lit Sut 1C 48
Dale Dr. CH65: Gt Sut 2F 49
Dale End Rd. CH61: Barn ...5E 27
Dale Gdns. CH60: Hes 2H 31
  CH65: Whit 4H 49
Dale Hey CH44: Wall 2F 13
  CH66: Hoot 3G 41
Dalehurst Cl. CH44: Wall ...1H 13
Dale Rd. CH62: Brom 5B 36
DALES, THE 3A 32
Daleside Cl. CH61: Irby 3B 26
Dale St. L2: Liv 3E 15
  L3: Liv 3F 15
Dalesway CH60: Hes 3A 32
Dale Vw. Cl. CH61: Pens ...5C 26
Dalmorton Rd.
  CH45: New B 3F 5
Dalrymple St. L5: Liv 6F 7
Dalton Rd. CH45: New B ...4G 5
Damhead La. CH64: Will ...6H 39
Danby Cl. L5: Liv 6H 7

Dane Cl.—Dunraven Rd.

Dane Cl. CH61: Irby 3B **26**
Danefield Rd. CH49: Grea 5C **18**
Danehurst Rd. CH45: Wall 4D **4**
Danescourt Rd. CH41: Birk 5E **13**
Dane St. L4: Walt 2H **7**
Daneswell Dr. CH46: More 4F **11**
Danger La. CH46: More 3F **11**
Daniel Ho. L20: Boot 1E **7**
Dansie St. L3: Liv 3G **15**
Darby Cl. CH64: Lit N 3C **44**
D'Arcy Cotts. *CH63: Thorn H 5B **34***
(off Raby Rd.)
Daresbury Rd. CH44: Wall 1E **13**
Darleydale Dr. CH62: East 6D **36**
Darlington Cl. CH44: Wall 1H **13**
Darlington St. CH44: Wall 1H **13**
Darmond's Grn. CH48: W Kir 4D **16**
Darnley St. L8: Liv 2G **23**
Darwen St. L5: Liv 6D **6**
Daryl Rd. CH60: Hes 2C **32**
Daulby St. L3: Liv 3H **15**
Davenham Av. CH43: O'ton 4D **20**
Davenham Cl. CH43: O'ton 5D **20**
Davenport Cl. CH48: Caldy 3B **24**
Davenport Rd. CH60: Hes 4A **32**
Daventree Rd. CH45: Wall 6F **5**
David Lloyd Leisure Cheshire Oaks 6B **50**
David St. L8: Liv 3H **23**
Davies St. L1: Liv 3E **15**
Davis Rd. CH46: Leas 2H **11**
Davy St. L5: Liv 5H **7**
Dawlish Rd. CH44: Wall 1D **12**
CH61: Irby 4G **25**
Dawn Cl. CH64: Ness 2E **45**
Dawn Gdns. CH65: Whit 3H **49**
Dawpool Cotts. CH48: Caldy 3E **25**
Dawpool Dr. CH46: More 5E **11**
CH62: Brom 4A **36**
Dawson Av. CH41: Birk 5F **13**
Dawson St. L1: Liv 3F **15**
Dawson Way *L1: Liv 4F **15***
(off St Johns Cen.)
Dawstone Ri. CH60: Hes 4B **32**
Dawstone Rd. CH60: Hes 4B **32**
Days Mdw. CH49: Grea 4C **18**
Deakin St. CH41: Birk 5D **12**
Dean Av. CH45: Wall 5C **4**
Dean Dillistone Ct. L1: Liv 6G **15**
Dean Patey Ct. L1: Liv 5G **15**
Deansgate CH65: Ell P 2G **49**
Deans Rd. CH65: Ell P 4D **50**
Deans Way CH41: Birk 5D **12**
Dearnford Av. CH62: Brom 5B **36**
Dearnford Cl. CH62: Brom 5B **36**
Debra Cl. CH66: Gt Sut 3C **48**
Debra Rd. CH66: Gt Sut 3C **48**
Deelands Pk. CH46: More 4C **10**
Dee La. CH48: W Kir 5C **16**
Dee Pk. Cl. CH60: Hes 5D **32**
Dee Pk. Rd. CH60: Hes 5D **32**
Deepdale Cl. CH43: Bid 1A **20**
Deerwood Cl. CH66: Lit Sut 6D **42**
Deerwood Cres. CH66: Lit Sut 6D **42**
Dee Sailing Club 4C **24**
Deeside CH60: Hes 3G **31**
CH65: Whit 4H **49**
Deeside Cl. CH43: Bid 1H **19**
CH65: Whit 5H **49**
Deeside Ct. CH64: Park 4A **38**
Deeview Ct. CH64: Nest 1C **44**
Dee Vw. Rd. CH60: Hes 3B **32**
De Grouchy St. CH48: W Kir 4D **16**
Delamere Av. CH62: East 1G **41**
CH66: Gt Sut 2E **49**
Delamere Cl. CH43: Bid 1A **20**
CH62: East 1G **41**
Delamere Dr. CH66: Gt Sut 3E **49**
Delamere Grn. CH66: Gt Sut 2E **49**
Delamere Gro. CH44: Wall 3A **14**
Delamore Pl. L4: Kirk 2G **7**
Delamore's Acre CH64: Will 5C **40**
Delamore St. L4: Kirk 2G **7**
Delavor Cl. CH60: Hes 3A **32**
Delavor Rd. CH60: Hes 3A **32**
Delf La. L4: Walt 1H **7**
Dell, The CH42: R Ferr 6C **22**
Dell Cl. CH63: Brom 5H **35**
Dell Ct. CH43: Pren 6D **20**
Dell Gro. CH42: R Ferr 1G **29**
Dell La. CH60: Hes 4D **32**
Delta Rd. E. CH42: R Ferr 6D **22**
Delta Rd. W. CH42: R Ferr 6D **22**
Delves Av. CH63: Spit 6F **29**
Delyn Cl. CH42: R Ferr 6A **22**
Demage Dr. CH66: Gt Sut 4D **48**
Demesne St. CH44: Wall 2A **14**
Denbigh Ct. CH65: Ell P 4B **50**
Denbigh Gdns. CH65: Ell P 4A **50**
Denbigh Rd. CH44: Wall 2G **13**
L9: Walt 1H **7**
Denbigh St. L5: Liv 6D **6**
Deneshey Rd. CH47: Meols 5E **9**
Denhall La. CH64: Burt 5E **45**
Denman Gro. CH44: Wall 3A **14**
Denning Dr. CH61: Irby 2H **25**
Denny Cl. CH49: Upton 3F **19**
Denston Cl. CH43: Bid 6H **11**
Dentdale Dr. L5: Liv 1G **15**
Denton Dr. CH45: Wall 5G **5**
Denton St. L8: Liv 3H **23**
Dentwood St. L8: Liv 3H **23**
Denwall Ho. CH64: Nest 5C **38**
Derby Rd. CH42: Tran 4H **21**
CH45: Wall 5E **5**
L5: Kirk 5D **6**
L20: Boot 1D **6**
Derby Sq. L2: Liv 4E **15**
Dereham Av. CH49: Upton 6G **11**
Derwent Cl. CH63: High B 4D **28**
Derwent Dr. CH45: Wall 5E **5**
CH61: Pens 5B **26**
CH66: Hoot 3B **42**
Derwent Rd. CH43: O'ton 3F **21**
CH47: Meols 5G **9**
CH63: High B 4D **28**
Derwent Way CH64: Lit N 6D **38**
Desford Cl. CH46: More 4B **10**
Desmond Cl. CH43: Bid 6A **12**
Deva Rd. CH48: W Kir 5C **16**
Deveraux Dr. CH44: Wall 2F **13**
Deverill Rd. CH42: R Ferr 6A **22**
Devisdale Gro. CH43: Bid 6A **12**
Devizes Dr. CH61: Irby 2H **25**
Devon Av. CH45: Wall 6G **5**
Devon Dr. CH61: Pens 5A **26**
Devon Gdns. CH42: R Ferr 6A **22**
Devonport St. L8: Liv 2H **23**
Devonshire Cl. CH43: O'ton 2F **21**
DEVONSHIRE PARK 4G **21**
Devonshire Pl. CH43: O'ton 2E **21**
L5: Liv 5G **7**
(not continuous)
Devonshire Rd. CH43: O'ton 2F **21**
CH44: Wall 1F **13**
CH48: W Kir 6E **17**
CH49: Upton 2E **19**
CH61: Pens 5A **26**
Devonshire Rd. W. L8: Liv 2H **23**
Devon St. L3: Liv 3G **15**
Dewberry Cl. CH42: Tran 3H **21**
Dexter St. L8: Liv 1G **23**
Dial Rd. CH42: Tran 4H **21**
Diamond St. L5: Liv 1F **15**
Diana St. L4: Walt 3H **7**
Diane Ho. *L8: Liv 6H **15***
(off Birley Ct.)
Dibbinsdale Local Nature Reserve 1A **36**
Dibbinsdale Rd. CH63: Brom 3H **35**
Dibbins Grn. CH63: Brom 5H **35**
Dibbins Hey CH63: Spit 1G **35**
Dibbinview Gro. CH63: Spit 1H **35**
Dickens Av. CH43: Pren 6D **20**
Dickens Cl. CH43: Pren 6D **20**
Dickenson St. *L1: Liv 5F **15***
(off Up. Frederick St.)
Dickens St. L8: Liv 1H **23**
Dickson St. L3: Liv 1D **14**
Digg La. CH46: More 4D **10**
DINGLE 4H **23**
Dingle Brow L8: Liv 4H **23**
Dingle Grange L8: Liv 4H **23**
Dingle Gro. L8: Liv 3H **23**
Dingle La. L8: Liv 4H **23**
Dingle Mt. L8: Liv 4H **23**
Dingle Rd. CH42: Tran 3G **21**
L8: Liv 4H **23**
Dingle Ter. L8: Liv 3H **23**
Dingle Va. L8: Liv 4H **23**
Dingwall Dr. CH49: Grea 4E **19**
Dinmore Rd. CH44: Wall 1F **13**
Dinsdale Rd. CH62: Brom 1C **36**
Ditton La. CH46: Leas 2D **10**
Dobson St. L6: Liv 1H **15**
Dobson Wlk. L6: Liv 1H **15**
Dock Rd. CH41: Birk 3E **13**
Dock Rd. Nth. CH62: Port S 3A **30**
Dock Rd. Sth. CH62: Brom 5B **30**
Docks Link CH44: Wall 2D **12**
Dock St. CH65: Ell P 2G **43**
Dock Yd. Rd. CH65: Ell P 1B **50**
Dodd Av. CH49: Grea 4D **18**
Doddridge Rd. L8: Liv 2G **23**
Dodleston Cl. CH43: Noct 3B **20**
Doe's Mdw. Rd. CH63: Brom 4H **35**
Dolphin Cres. CH66: Gt Sut 5E **49**
Dombey Pl. L8: Liv 1H **23**
Dombey St. L8: Liv 1H **23**
Domville Dr. CH49: W'chu 4G **19**
Donaldson Ct. L5: Liv 5H **7**
Donaldson St. L5: Liv 5H **7**
Doncaster Dr. CH49: Upton 1F **19**
Donne Av. CH63: Spit 6F **29**
Donne Cl. CH63: Spit 6G **29**
Don Wlk. CH65: Ell P 6G **43**
Doon Cl. L4: Kirk 3G **7**
Dorans La. L2: Liv 4E **15**
Dorchester Cl. CH49: Upton 3F **19**
Dorchester Pk. CH43: Noct 4B **20**
Doreen Av. CH46: More 5D **10**
Doric St. CH42: R Ferr 5B **22**
Dorin Ct. CH43: O'ton 3E **21**
Dorrit St. L8: Liv 1H **23**
Dorset Dr. CH61: Pens 5A **26**
Dorset Gdns. CH42: R Ferr 6A **22**
Dorset Rd. CH45: New B 4E **5**
CH48: W Kir 4E **17**
Douglas Arc. *CH41: Birk 1A **22***
(off Douglas St.)
Douglas Dr. CH46: More 5D **10**
Douglas Pl. L20: Boot 1D **6**
Douglas Rd. CH48: W Kir 4F **17**
Douglas St. CH41: Birk 1A **22**
Doulton Cl. CH43: Bid 6H **11**
Doune Ct. CH65: Ell P 4B **50**
Douro St. L5: Liv 1G **15**
Dove Cl. CH66: Ell P 6G **43**
Dovedale Av. CH62: East 6C **36**
Dovedale Cl. CH43: Pren 5D **20**
Dovedale Rd. CH45: Wall 4E **5**
CH47: Hoy 5D **8**
Dovepoint Rd. CH47: Meols 4G **9**
Dover Cl. CH41: Birk 6H **13**
Dover Ct. CH65: Ell P 5B **50**
Dover Dr. CH65: Ell P 5B **50**
Dover St. L3: Liv 3H **15**
Dovesmead Rd. CH60: Hes 4F **33**
Dovey St. L8: Liv 2H **23**
Downes Grn. CH63: Spit 2G **35**
Downham Dr. CH60: Hes 3C **32**
Downham Rd. CH42: Tran 4H **21**
Downham Rd. Nth. CH61: Hes 1C **32**
Downham Rd. Sth. CH60: Hes 3C **32**
Downing Cl. CH43: O'ton 4F **21**
Downing Rd. L20: Boot 1F **7**
Downing St. L5: Liv 6H **7**
Drake Rd. CH46: Leas 1H **11**
CH64: Nest 4C **38**
Drake St. L20: Boot 2D **6**
Draycott St. L8: Liv 4H **23**
Drayton Cl. CH61: Irby 4H **25**
Drayton Rd. CH44: Wall 2G **13**
L4: Walt 1H **7**
Drinkwater Gdns. L3: Liv 2G **15**
Droitwich Av. CH49: Grea 3C **18**
Druids Way CH49: W'chu 5G **19**
Drummond Av. CH66: Gt Sut 3C **48**
Drummond Rd. CH47: Hoy 2C **16**
Drury La. L2: Liv 4E **15**
Dryburgh Way L4: Kirk 3G **7**
Dryden Cl. CH43: Bid 6A **12**
Dryden St. L5: Liv 1F **15**
Dryfield Cl. CH49: Grea 3D **18**
Dublin Cft. CH66: Gt Sut 6E **49**
Dublin St. L3: Liv 1D **14**
Duckinfield St. L3: Liv 4H **15**
Duck Pond La. CH42: Tran 5E **21**
Duddon Cl. CH43: O'ton 4D **20**
Dudleston Rd. CH66: Lit Sut 1B **48**
Dudley Cl. CH43: O'ton 3F **21**
Dudley Cres. CH65: Hoot 2B **42**
Dudley Rd. CH45: New B 3E **5**
CH65: Ell P 2H **49**
Duke of York Cotts. CH62: New F 3G **29**
Dukes Rd. L5: Liv 5G **7**
Dukes Ter. L1: Liv 5G **15**
Duke St. CH41: Birk 4G **13**
CH45: New B 3F **5**
L1: Liv 5F **15**
Duke St. Bri. CH41: Birk 4G **13**
Duke St. La. L1: Liv 5F **15**
Dumbarton St. L4: Walt 2G **7**
Dunbar Cl. CH66: Lit Sut 2C **48**
Dunbar Ct. CH66: Lit Sut 2C **48**
Dunbar St. L4: Walt 1H **7**
Duncan Dr. CH49: Grea 3D **18**
Duncansby Dr. CH63: East 1E **41**
Duncan St. CH41: Birk 1B **22**
L1: Liv 6G **15**
Duncote Cl. CH43: O'ton 3E **21**
Dundas St. L20: Boot 2D **6**
Dundee Ct. CH65: Ell P 4C **50**
Dundee Gro. CH44: Wall 2E **13**
Dundonald St. CH41: Birk 5E **13**
Dunes Way L5: Kirk 5E **7**
Dunham Cl. CH62: East 2H **41**
Dunkirk Cres. CH65: Whit 6G **49**
Dunkirk Dr. CH65: Whit 6H **49**
Dunkirk La. CH1: Dunk 6C **48**
CH65: Whit 6G **49**
Dunlins Ct. CH45: Wall 3C **4**
Dunluce St. L4: Walt 2G **7**
Dunmore Cres. CH66: Lit Sut 1B **48**
Dunmore Rd. CH66: Lit Sut 1B **48**
Dunnett St. L20: Kirk 2D **6**
Dunning Cl. CH49: Upton 2E **19**
Dunraven Rd. CH48: W Kir 5C **16**
CH64: Lit N 6E **39**

Dunstall Cl.—Fairview Av.

Dunstall Cl. CH46: Leas 2E **11**
Dunstan La. CH64: Burt 5A **46**
Dunster Gro. CH60: Hes 4D **32**
Durban Rd. CH45: Wall 5F **5**
Durham Ct. CH65: Ell P 4C **50**
Durley Dr. CH43: Pren 6C **20**
Durley Pk. Cl. CH43: Pren 1G **27**
Dutton Dr. CH63: Spit 1F **35**
Dutton Grn. CH2: Lit Stan 4D **50**
Dwerryhouse St.
L8: Liv 1F **23**
Dyke St. L6: Liv 1H **15**
Dyson St. L4: Walt 2H **7**

E

Eagle La. CH66: Lit Sut 6D **42**
Earle Cres. CH64: Nest 4B **38**
Earle Dr. CH64: Park 5B **38**
Earle Ho. CH62: New F 1H **29**
Earle St. L3: Liv 3E **15**
(not continuous)
Earls Gdns. CH65: Ell P 2H **49**
Earlston Rd. CH45: Wall 5E **5**
Earl St. CH62: New F 1H **29**
Earlswood Cl.
CH46: More 5B **10**
Easby Rd. L4: Kirk 4F **7**
(not continuous)
Easby Wlk. L4: Kirk 4F **7**
East Bank CH42: Tran 4G **21**
Eastbourne Rd.
CH41: Birk 1G **21**
Eastbourne Wlk.
L6: Liv 1H **15**
E. Brook St. L5: Liv 5H **7**
Eastcott Cl. CH49: Grea 4C **18**
Eastcroft Rd. CH44: Wall 2G **13**
Eastern Av. CH62: Brom 5B **30**
E. Farm M. CH48: Caldy 1D **24**
EASTHAM 6C **36**
EASTHAM FERRY 3E **37**
Eastham M. CH62: East 1A **42**
Eastham Rake CH62: East 2F **41**
CH66: East, Hoot 3E **41**
Eastham Rake Station (Rail)
. . . . .2F **41**
Eastham Village Rd.
CH62: East 6D **36**
Eastlake Av. L5: Liv 6H **7**
Eastleigh Dr. CH61: Irby 2H **25**
Easton Rd. CH62: New F 1H **29**
Eastpark Ct. CH44: Wall 2A **14**
East St. CH41: Birk 3A **14**
L3: Liv 3D **14**
Eastview Cl. CH43: Noct 3B **20**
East Way CH46: More 4E **11**
Eastway CH49: Grea 3E **19**
CH66: Lit Sut 6D **42**
Eastwood L17: Aig 4H **23**
Eaton Av. CH44: Wall 1G **13**
Eaton Rd. CH43: O'ton 2F **21**
CH48: W Kir 6C **16**
Eaton St. CH44: Wall 6F **5**
L3: Liv 2E **15**
Ebenezer St. CH42: R Ferr 5C **22**
Eberle St. L2: Liv 3E **15**
Ebony Cl. CH46: More 5B **10**
Ebor La. L5: Liv 1G **15**
Eccleshall Rd.
CH62: Port S 3A **30**
Eccleston Av. CH62: Brom 2A **36**
CH66: Ell P 2E **49**
Eccleston Cl. CH43: O'ton 4D **20**
Echo La. CH48: W Kir 6E **17**
Edale Cl. CH62: East 6C **36**
Eddisbury Rd. CH44: Wall 6G **5**
CH47: Hoy 3C **16**
CH48: W Kir 3C **16**
CH66: Whit 5F **49**
Eden Cl. CH66: Gt Sut 2C **48**
Edenhurst Av. CH44: Wall 6G **5**
Edenpark Rd. CH42: Tran 4G **21**
Edgar Ct. CH41: Birk 6H **13**
Edgar St. CH41: Birk 6H **13**
L3: Liv 2F **15**
Edgbaston Way CH43: Bid 5A **12**
Edgefield Cl. CH43: Noct 3B **20**
Edgehill Rd. CH46: More 5C **10**
Edgemoor Cl. CH43: Bid 6H **11**
Edgemoor Dr. CH61: Irby 2G **25**
Edgewood Dr.
CH62: Brom 6B **36**
Edgewood Rd.
CH47: Meols 4F **9**
CH49: Upton 1F **19**
Edinburgh Ct. CH65: Ell P 4B **50**
Edinburgh Dr. CH43: Pren 6E **21**
Edinburgh Rd. CH45: Wall 6F **5**
L7: Liv 3H **15**
Edith Rd. CH44: Wall 2H **13**
Edmonton Cl. L5: Kirk 5F **7**
Edmund St. L3: Liv 3E **15**
Edrich Av. CH43: Bid 5A **12**
Edward Pav. L3: Liv 5E **15**
Edward Rd. CH47: Hoy 1E **17**
Edward St. CH65: Ell P 2G **43**
L3: Liv 4G **15**
Effingham St. L20: Boot 1D **6**
Egan Rd. CH43: Bid 5C **12**
Egbert Rd. CH47: Meols 5E **9**
Egerton Dr. CH48: W Kir 5D **16**
Egerton Gdns.
CH42: R Ferr 6A **22**
Egerton Gro. CH45: Wall 6F **5**
Egerton Pk. CH42: R Ferr 6A **22**
Egerton Pk. Cl.
CH42: R Ferr 6A **22**
Egerton Rd. CH43: C'ton 1E **21**
CH62: New F 2H **29**
Egerton St. CH45: New B 3F **5**
CH65: Ell P 1A **50**
L8: Liv 6H **15**
Egerton Wharf CH41: Birk 6A **14**
EGREMONT 6H **5**
Egremont Prom.
CH44: Wall 5H **5**
CH45: Wall 5H **5**
Elaine Cl. CH66: Gt Sut 3C **48**
Elaine Norris Sports Cen. 1E **15**
Elaine St. L8: Liv 1H **23**
Elder Gro. CH48: W Kir 5D **16**
Elderwood Rd.
CH42: Tran 4A **22**
Eldon Gro. L3: Liv 1F **15**
Eldonian Way L3: Liv 1E **15**
Eldon Pl. L3: Liv 1E **15**
Eldon Rd. CH42: R Ferr 5B **22**
CH44: Wall 1F **13**
Eldon St. L3: Liv 1E **15**
Eldon Ter. CH64: Nest 6C **38**
Eleanor Pk. CH43: Bid 5A **12**
Eleanor Rd. CH43: Bid 4B **12**
CH46: More 4D **10**
Eleanor St. CH65: Ell P 1A **50**
L20: Kirk 2D **6**
Elfet St. CH41: Birk 5D **12**
Elgar Av. CH62: East 6C **36**
Elgar Cl. CH65: Gt Sut 4F **49**
Elgin Dr. CH45: Wall 5G **5**
Elgin Way CH41: Birk 6A **14**
Eliot Cl. CH62: New F 2G **29**
Elizabeth St. L3: Liv 3H **15**
Elland Dr. CH66: Lit Sut 2C **48**
Ellens Cl. L6: Liv 3H **15**
Ellen's La. CH63: Beb 4G **29**
Elleray Dr. L8: Liv 3H **23**
Elleray Pk. Rd. CH45: Wall 4E **5**
Ellerman Rd. L3: Liv 4G **23**
Ellerton Av. CH66: Lit Sut 2C **48**
Ellesmere Gro. CH45: Wall 5F **5**
ELLESMERE PORT 2A **50**
ELLESMERE PORT HOSPITAL
. . . . .5G **49**
Ellesmere Port Stadium 4C **50**
Ellesmere Port Station (Rail)
. . . . .2A **50**
Elliot St. L1: Liv 4F **15**
Ellis Pl. L8: Liv 2H **23**
Elm Av. CH49: Upton 1D **18**
Elm Bank L4: Walt 4H **7**
Elmbank Rd.
CH62: New F 3H **29**
Elmbank St. CH44: Wall 2G **13**
Elm Cl. CH61: Pens 5C **26**
Elm Ct. CH63: High B 3D **28**
Elmdene Ct. CH49: Grea 5C **18**
Elm Dr. CH49: Grea 4C **18**
Elm Grn. CH64: Will 5B **40**
Elm Gro. CH42: Tran 3H **21**
CH47: Hoy 6E **9**
CH66: Whit 6G **49**
L7: Liv 4H **15**
Elmore Cl. L5: Liv 6H **7**
Elm Pk. Rd. CH45: Wall 4E **5**
Elm Rd. CH42: Tran 4H **21**
(Derby Rd.)
CH42: Tran 5F **21**
(Waterpark Rd.)
CH61: Irby 3B **26**
CH63: High B 2F **29**
CH64: Will 5B **40**
Elm Rd. Nth. CH42: Tran 5F **21**
Elms Pk. CH61: Thing 4C **26**
Elm St. CH41: Birk 1H **21**
CH65: Ell P 2G **43**
Elmswood Rd.
CH42: Tran 3G **21**
CH44: Wall 1H **13**
Elm Ter. CH47: Hoy 6E **9**
Elmtree Gro. CH43: Bid 5C **12**
Elmure Av. CH63: High B 4D **28**
Elmwood Dr. CH61: Hes 1B **32**
Elphin Gro. L4: Walt 2H **7**
Elstow St. L5: Kirk 4F **7**
Elswick St. L8: Liv 4H **23**
Eltham Cl. CH49: W'chu 5H **19**
Eltham Grn. CH49: W'chu 5H **19**
Elton Cl. CH62: East 2G **41**
Elton Dr. CH63: Spit 6G **29**
Elton St. L4: Walt 1H **7**
Elwyn Rd. CH47: Meols 4G **9**
Elwy St. L8: Liv 2H **23**
Ely Av. CH46: More 5C **10**
Ember Cres. L6: Liv 1H **15**
Emerald St. L8: Liv 4H **23**
Emerson St. L8: Liv 6H **15**
Emery St. L4: Walt 2H **7**
Empire Bri. *L3: Liv 3D **14***
(off Union St.)
Empress Rd. CH44: Wall 1G **13**
Emslie Ct. CH64: Park 6A **38**
Enerby Cl. CH43: Bid 6A **12**
Enfield Rd. CH65: Ell P 2H **49**
Enfield Ter. CH43: O'ton 2F **21**
Enid St. L8: Liv 1H **23**
Ennerdale Av. CH62: East 1H **41**
Ennerdale Rd.
CH43: Pren 6C **20**
CH45: Wall 3D **4**
Ennerdale St. L3: Liv 1F **15**
Ennisdale Dr. CH48: W Kir 4F **17**
Ensor St. L20: Boot 2D **6**
Enterprise Pk. CH65: Ell P 3C **50**
EPIC Leisure Cen. 3H **49**
Epping Ct. CH60: Hes 3C **32**
Epsom Rd. CH46: Leas 2F **11**
Epsom Way L5: Liv 6F **7**
Epworth Cl. CH43: C'ton 1E **21**
Epworth Grange
*CH43: C'ton 1E **21***
(off Park Rd. W.)
Epworth St. L6: Liv 3H **15**
Erfurt Av. CH63: Beb 5G **29**
Erica Ct. CH60: Hes 2A **32**
Eric Fountain Rd.
CH65: Ell P 2D **42**
Eric Gro. CH44: Wall 1E **13**
Eric Rd. CH44: Wall 1E **13**
Eridge St. L8: Liv 3H **23**
Erin Cl. L8: Liv 1G **23**
Ermine Cres. L5: Liv 6H **7**
Errington Av. CH65: Ell P 1A **50**
Errington St. L5: Kirk 5D **6**
Erskine Ind. Est.
L6: Liv 2H **15**
Erskine Rd. CH44: Wall 2G **13**
Erskine St. L6: Liv 2H **15**
Erskine St. Ind. Est.
*L6: Liv 3H **15***
(off Erskine St.)
Escolme Dr. CH49: Grea 4D **18**
Esher Cl. CH43: Bid 6A **12**
CH62: New F 1H **29**
Esher Rd. CH62: New F 1H **29**
Eskdale CH65: Whit 4H **49**
Eskdale Av. CH46: More 4C **10**
CH62: East 6C **36**
Esk St. L20: Kirk 3D **6**
Espin St. L4: Walt 2H **7**
Esplanade CH42: R Ferr 5C **22**
Esplanade, The
CH62: New F 6D **22**
Essex Rd. CH48: W Kir 4E **17**
Essex St. L8: Liv 2G **23**
Ethelbert Rd. CH47: Meols 5E **9**
Ethel Rd. CH44: Wall 2H **13**
Eton Dr. CH63: Thorn H 5H **33**
Eton Rd. CH65: Ell P 3B **50**
Eton St. L4: Walt 2H **7**
Europa Blvd. CH41: Birk 1A **22**
Europa Cen., The
CH41: Birk 1H **21**
Europa Pools 6H **13**
Europa Sq. CH41: Birk 1H **21**
Europa Way CH65: Ell P 1A **50**
Euston Gro. CH43: O'ton 2F **21**
Euston St. L4: Walt 1H **7**
Evans Rd. CH47: Hoy 6D **8**
Evelyn Rd. CH44: Wall 2G **13**
Evelyn St. L5: Kirk 5F **7**
Everest Cl. CH66: Gt Sut 4F **49**
Everest Rd. CH42: Tran 5H **21**
Evergreen Cl.
CH49: Upton 1E **19**
Everleigh Cl. CH43: Bid 6A **12**
Eversleigh Dr. CH63: Beb 5G **29**
Eversley Pk. CH43: O'ton 4F **21**
Eversley St. L8: Liv 1H **23**
(not continuous)
EVERTON 6G **7**
Everton Brow L3: Liv 2G **15**
Everton FC 2H **7**
Everton Pk. Sports Cen. 6G **7**
Everton Rd. L6: Liv 1H **15**
Everton Valley L4: Walt 4G **7**
Everton Vw. L20: Boot 1D **6**
Everyman Theatre 4H **15**
Evesham Rd. CH45: Wall 5D **4**
Ewloe Ct. CH65: Ell P 5B **50**
Exchange Flags *L2: Liv 3E **15***
(off Exchange Pas. W.)
Exchange Pas. E. L2: Liv 3E **15**
Exchange Pas. W. L2: Liv 3E **15**
Exchange St. E. L2: Liv 3E **15**
Exchange St. W. L2: Liv 3E **15**
Exeter Rd. CH44: Wall 6G **5**
CH65: Ell P 2A **50**
L20: Boot 1E **7**
Exmoor Cl. CH61: Pens 4B **26**
Exmouth Cl. CH41: Birk 1H **21**
Exmouth Gdns. CH41: Birk . . .1H **21**
Exmouth St. CH41: Birk 1H **21**
Exmouth Way CH41: Birk 1H **21**

F

FACT Cen. 5F **15**
Fairacres Rd. CH63: Beb 5F **29**
Fairbeech Ct. CH43: Bid 6A **12**
Fairbeech M. CH43: Bid 6A **12**
Fairbrook Dr. CH41: Birk 4C **12**
Fairclough La.
CH43: O'ton 3F **21**
Fairclough St. L1: Liv 4F **15**
Fairfax Rd. CH41: Tran 3A **22**
Fairfield Av. CH65: Whit 5G **49**
Fairfield Cres.
CH46: More 5D **10**
Fairfield Dr. CH48: W Kir 4G **17**
Fairfield Rd. CH42: Tran 5A **22**
Fairhaven Cl.
CH42: R Ferr 5B **22**
Fairhaven Dr.
CH63: Brom 6A **36**
Fairholme Av. CH64: Nest 4B **38**
Fair Isle Cl. CH65: Ell P 6A **50**
Fairlawn Cl.
CH63: Raby M 5G **35**
Fairlawn Ct. CH43: O'ton 2D **20**
Fairmead Rd. CH46: More 4E **11**
Fairoak Cl. CH43: Bid 6A **12**
Fair Vw. CH41: Tran 3A **22**
Fairview Av. CH45: Wall 6E **5**

Fairview Cl.—Gayton La.

Fairview Cl. CH43: O'ton 4F **21**
Fairview Rd. CH43: O'ton 5F **21**
CH65: Whit 5G **49**
Fairview Way CH61: Pens 6B **26**
Fairway Cres.
CH62: Brom 5B **30**
Fairway Nth. CH62: Brom 5B **30**
Fairways CH42: Tran 1B **28**
Fairways, The
CH48: Caldy 3B **24**
Fairways Dr.
CH66: Lit Sut 5D **42**
Fairway Sth. CH62: Brom 6B **30**
Falcongate Ind. Est.
*CH44: Wall 4G **13***
(off Old Gorsey La.)
Falcon Rd. CH41: Birk 3G **21**
CH66: Gt Sut 4F **49**
Falkland Rd. CH44: Wall 1H **13**
Falkland St. CH41: Birk 5E **13**
L3: Liv 3H **15**
(not continuous)
Falkner Sq. L8: Liv 5H **15**
Falkner St. L7: Liv 5H **15**
L8: Liv 5H **15**
(not continuous)
Falkner Ter. *L8: Liv 6H **15***
(off Up. Parliament St.)
Fallowfield Rd.
CH46: More 5G **11**
Falstaff St. L20: Kirk 2E **7**
Faraday Rd. CH65: Whit 3G **49**
Faraday St. L5: Liv 6H **7**
Fareham Cl. CH49: Upton 1E **19**
Farley Av. CH62: Brom 2A **36**
Farlow Rd. CH42: R Ferr 6B **22**
Farm Cl. CH49: Grea 3C **18**
Far Mdw. La. CH61: Irby 3G **25**
Farmers Heath
CH66: Gt Sut 5D **48**
Farmfield Dr. CH43: Bid 6A **12**
Farmside CH46: Leas 2F **11**
Farmstead Way
CH66: Gt Sut 6E **49**
Farndon Av. CH45: Wall 5C **4**
Farndon Dr. CH48: W Kir 4G **17**
Farndon Rd. CH66: Ell P 1E **49**
Farndon Way CH43: O'ton 3D **20**
Farne Cl. CH65: Ell P 6A **50**
Farnworth Av. CH46: Leas 1F **11**
Farr Hall Dr. CH60: Hes 4A **32**
Farr Hall Rd. CH60: Hes 3A **32**
Farriers Way CH48: Frank 5B **18**
Fazakerley Bri. *L3: Liv 3D **14***
(off Fazakerley St.)
Fazakerley St. L3: Liv 3D **14**
Fearnley Hall CH41: Birk 2H **21**
Fearnley Rd. CH41: Birk 2H **21**
Feather La. CH60: Hes 3B **32**
(not continuous)
Feilden Rd. CH63: Beb 5G **29**
Felicity Gro. CH46: More 4D **10**
Fell St. CH44: Wall 3A **14**
Felthorpe Cl.
CH49: Upton 6H **11**
Felton Cl. CH46: More 5C **10**
Feltree Ho. CH43: Bid 6A **12**
Fendale Av. CH46: More 4G **11**
Fender Ct. CH49: W'chu 6B **20**
Fender La. CH43: Bid 4G **11**
CH46: More 4G **11**
Fenderside Rd. CH43: Bid 5A **12**
Fender Vw. Rd.
CH46: More 5G **11**
Fender Way CH43: Bid 6H **11**
Fenderway CH61: Pens 5C **26**
Fenwick Rd. CH66: Gt Sut 5E **49**
Fenwick St. L2: Liv 4E **15**
Ferguson Av. CH49: Grea 4D **18**
CH66: Ell P 1E **49**
Fernbank La.
CH49: Upton 6F **11**
Ferndale Av. CH44: Wall 1G **13**
CH48: Frank 6B **18**
Ferndale Rd. CH47: Hoy 6D **8**
Fern Gro. CH43: Noct 2B **20**
Fernhill CH45: New B 3F **5**
Fernhill Cl. L20: Boot 1G **7**
(not continuous)
Fernhill Dr. L8: Liv 1H **23**
Fernhill Gdns. L20: Boot 1G **7**
Fernhill M. E. L20: Boot 1G **7**
Fernhill M. W. L20: Boot 1G **7**
Fernhill Rd. L20: Boot 1G **7**
Fernhill Way L20: Boot 1G **7**
Fernie Cres. L8: Liv 2G **23**
Fernlea M. CH43: Bid 5A **12**
Fernlea Rd. CH60: Hes 3C **32**
Fernleigh CH43: O'ton 4F **21**
Fern Rd. CH65: Whit 5G **49**
Ferns Cl. CH60: Hes 2G **31**
Ferns Rd. CH63: High B 4D **28**
Ferny Brow Rd.
CH49: W'chu 4H **19**
Fernyess La. CH64: Will 1A **46**
Ferries Cl. CH42: R Ferr 1G **29**
Ferry Rd. CH62: East 6E **37**
Ferryside CH44: Wall 3A **14**
Ferry Vw. Rd. CH44: Wall 3A **14**
Festival Rd. CH65: Ell P 2F **49**
Ffrancon Dr. CH63: High B 2F **29**
Field Cl. CH62: New F 1H **29**
Field Hey La. CH64: Will 4D **40**
(not continuous)
Field Rd. CH45: New B 4F **5**
Fieldside Rd.
CH42: R Ferr 5A **22**
Field St. L3: Liv 2G **15**
(not continuous)
Fieldway CH45: Wall 6E **5**
CH47: Meols 6H **9**
CH60: Hes 2E **33**
CH63: High B 1D **28**
CH66: Lit Sut 6B **42**
Fieldway Ct. CH41: Birk 5G **13**
Fifth Av. CH43: Bid 6H **11**
Finch Ct. CH41: Birk 6H **13**
Finchdean Cl. CH49: Grea 4C **18**
Finch Pl. L3: Liv 3H **15**
Findley Dr. CH46: Leas 2F **11**
Finney, The CH48: Caldy 3B **24**
Finstall Rd. CH63: Spit 1F **35**
Firbrook Ct. CH43: Bid 4A **12**
Firdene Cres. CH43: Noct 3C **20**
Firs, The CH43: Bid 5C **12**
Firs Av. CH63: Beb 6F **29**
Firshaw Rd. CH47: Meols 4E **9**
First Av. CH43: Bid 1A **20**
Firtree Gro. CH66: Whit 6B **48**
Fir Way CH60: Hes 6D **32**
Fishers La. CH61: Pens 5A **26**
Fisher St. L8: Liv 1F **23**
Fishguard Cl. L6: Liv 1H **15**
Fitness First
Bromborough 6C **30**
Fitzclarence Wlk. L6: Liv 1H **15**
Fitzclarence Way L6: Liv 1H **15**
Fitzpatrick Ct. L3: Liv 1E **15**
Fitzroy Way L6: Liv 2H **15**
Fiveways Pk. CH64: Nest 2D **38**
Flag La. CH64: Lit N 6D **38**
Flail Cl. CH49: Grea 3D **18**
Flambards CH49: W'chu 4A **20**
Flashes La. CH64: Ness 2F **45**
Flatt La. CH43: O'ton 4D **20**
CH65: Ell P 2H **49**
Flaxhill CH46: More 4D **10**
Flaybrick Cl. CH43: Bid 5C **12**
Fleck La.
CH48: Caldy, W Kir 6F **17**
Fleet Cft. Rd.
CH49: W'chu 5G **19**
Fleet St. CH65: Ell P 2G **49**
L1: Liv 4F **15**
Fleming Ct. L3: Liv 1E **15**
Fleming St. CH65: Ell P 1A **50**
Fleming Way CH46: Leas 3G **11**
Fletcher Av. CH42: R Ferr 5A **22**
Fletcher Cl. CH49: W'chu 5G **19**
Flint Cl. CH64: Nest 1C **44**
Flint Ct. CH65: Ell P 5B **50**
Flint Dr. CH64: Nest 6C **38**
Flint Mdw. CH64: Nest 6C **38**
Flint St. L1: Liv 6F **15**
Floral Pavilion Theatre 2G **5**
Floral Wood L17: Aig 5H **23**
Florence Av. CH60: Hes 2B **32**
Florence Rd. CH44: Wall 2A **14**
Florence St. CH41: Birk 1H **21**
L4: Walt 3H **7**
Flowermead Cl.
CH47: Meols 4H **9**
Folds, The CH63: Thorn H 5A **34**
Foley Cl. L4: Kirk 4G **7**
Foley St. L4: Kirk 4G **7**
(not continuous)
Folly La. CH44: Wall 6C **4**
Fontenoy St. L3: Liv 3F **15**
Fonthill Cl. L4: Kirk 4F **7**
Fonthill Rd. L4: Kirk 3F **7**
FORD **2A 20**
Ford Cl. CH49: Upton 3H **19**
Ford Dr. CH49: Upton 2H **19**
Fordham St. L4: Kirk 3G **7**
Fordhill Vw. CH46: More 5G **11**
Ford La. CH49: Upton 2H **19**
Ford Rd. CH49: Upton 2G **19**
Ford St. L3: Liv 2E **15**
Ford Way CH49: Upton 3G **19**
Fordway M.
CH49: Upton 3G **19**
Forest Cl. CH47: Meols 4F **9**
Forest Ct. CH43: C'ton 1D **20**
Forest Rd. CH43: C'ton 6E **13**
CH47: Meols 4F **9**
CH60: Hes 2C **32**
CH66: Ell P 6E **43**
Forge Rd. CH66: Lit Sut 1C **48**
Forge St. L20: Kirk 3E **7**
Fornalls Grn. La.
CH47: Meols 6G **9**
Forrest St. L1: Liv 5F **15**
Forth St. L20: Kirk 2D **6**
Fort Perch Rock 2G **5**
Fort St. CH45: New B 4G **5**
Forwood Rd. CH62: Brom 3B **36**
Foster St. L20: Kirk 4E **7**
Fotheringay Ct.
CH65: Ell P 5B **50**
Fountain Rd. CH45: New B 4F **5**
Fountains Cl. L4: Walt 4H **7**
Fountains Ct. L5: Kirk 4F **7**
Fountains Rd. L4: Kirk 4F **7**
(not continuous)
Fountain St. CH42: Tran 4G **21**
Four Bridges CH41: Birk 5A **14**
Fourth Av. CH43: Bid 6H **11**
Fowell Rd. CH45: New B 3F **5**
Foxall Way CH66: Gt Sut 5C **48**
Foxcover Rd. CH60: Hes 4E **33**
Foxcovers Rd. CH63: Beb 6G **29**
Foxdale Cl. CH43: O'ton 2E **21**
Foxdene CH66: Lit Sut 2D **48**
Foxes, The CH61: Thing 3D **26**
Foxfield Rd. CH47: Meols 5F **9**
Foxglove Rd. CH41: Birk 6D **12**
Foxglove Way CH64: Lit N 2C **44**
Fox Hey Rd. CH44: Wall 1D **12**
Foxhill Cl. L8: Liv 1H **23**
Foxleigh Grange
CH41: Birk 4D **12**
Fox St. CH41: Birk 1G **21**
L3: Liv 1G **15**
Foxton Cl. CH46: More 4B **10**
Foxwood Cl. CH48: W Kir 4G **17**
Franceys St. L3: Liv 4G **15**
Francine Cl. L3: Liv 6E **7**
Francis Av. CH43: C'ton 1F **21**
CH46: More 5D **10**
FRANKBY **5B 18**
Frankby Av. CH44: Wall 1E **13**
Frankby Cl. CH49: Grea 4B **18**
Frankby Grn. CH48: Frank 5B **18**
Frankby Gro. CH49: Upton 2F **19**
Frankby Rd. CH47: Meols 5F **9**
CH48: Frank, W Kir 4F **17**
CH49: Grea 4F **17**
Frankby Stiles
CH48: Frank 4H **17**
Franklin Rd. CH46: Leas 1G **11**
Frank St. L8: Liv 2G **23**
Fraser St. L3: Liv 3G **15**
Frederick St. *L1: Liv 5E **15***
(off Cleveland Bldgs.)
Freedom Cl. L7: Liv 5H **15**
Freeland St. L4: Kirk 4G **7**
Freeman St. CH41: Birk 6A **14**
Freemason's Row L3: Liv 2E **15**
(not continuous)
Frensham Cl. CH63: Spit 1F **35**
Friars Cl. CH63: Beb 4F **29**
Frobisher Rd. CH46: Leas 1G **11**
CH64: Nest 5C **38**
Frodsham St. CH41: Tran 3A **22**
(not continuous)
L4: Walt 2H **7**
Frome Cl. CH61: Irby 2H **25**
Frome Ct. CH65: Ell P 6H **43**
Frost Dr. CH61: Irby 3G **25**
Frosts M. CH65: Ell P 1H **49**
Fuchsia Cl. CH66: Gt Sut 6F **49**
Fuchsia Wlk. CH49: Grea 5C **18**
Fulbrook Cl. CH63: Spit 6F **29**
Fulbrook Rd. CH63: Spit 1F **35**
Fulford Pk. CH46: More 5E **11**
Fulton Av. CH48: W Kir 4G **17**
Fulton St. L5: Liv 6D **6**
Fulwood Gdns.
CH66: Lit Sut 1C **48**
Fulwood M. CH66: Lit Sut 1C **48**
Fulwood Rd.
CH66: Lit Sut 1C **48**
Furness Cl. CH49: Upton 1E **19**
Furness St. L4: Walt 4G **7**
Furrocks Cl. CH64: Ness 2D **44**
Furrocks La. CH64: Ness 2D **44**
Furrocks Way CH64: Ness 2D **44**
Furrows, The
CH66: Gt Sut 6A **48**
Furze Way CH46: More 4E **11**

G

Gabriel Cl. CH46: More 5F **11**
Gainsborough Rd.
CH45: Wall 6C **4**
CH49: Upton 1F **19**
Gala Bingo
Bromborough 6C **30**
Gallagher Ind. Est.
CH41: Birk 4F **13**
Gallopers La.
CH61: Thing 3E **27**
Galton St. L3: Liv 2D **14**
Galtres Ct. CH63: High B 1E **29**
Galtres Pk. CH63: High B 1E **29**
Gambier Ter. L1: Liv 6G **15**
Gamlin St. CH41: Birk 5D **12**
Ganney's Mdw. Rd.
CH49: W'chu 5A **20**
Garden Ct. CH42: Tran 6G **21**
Garden Hey Rd.
CH46: More 6B **10**
CH47: Meols 5E **9**
Gardenia Gro. L17: Aig 5H **23**
Garden La. CH46: More 4E **11**
L5: Liv 1G **15**
Gardenside CH46: Leas 1H **11**
Gardenside St. L6: Liv 2H **15**
Gardens Rd. CH63: Beb 4H **29**
Gardner's Row L3: Liv 2F **15**
Garfield Ter. CH49: Upton 2G **19**
Garnett Av. L4: Kirk 3F **7**
Garnge Wood
CH48: W Kir 6F **17**
Garrick Av. CH46: More 5C **10**
Garrick Rd. CH43: Pren 1H **27**
Garswood Cl. CH46: Leas 1F **11**
Garswood St. L8: Liv 4H **23**
Garth Blvd. CH63: High B 1E **29**
Garth Rd. CH65: Ell P 2D **50**
Gascoyne St. L3: Liv 2E **15**
Gateacre Ct. CH66: Ell P 5F **43**
Gautby Rd. CH41: Birk 4C **12**
Gawsworth Cl.
CH43: O'ton 4D **20**
Gawsworth Rd.
CH66: Gt Sut 2E **49**
Gaybeech Cl. CH43: Bid 5H **11**
GAYTON **4D 32**
Gayton Av. CH45: New B 3F **5**
CH63: High B 1C **28**
Gayton Farm Rd.
CH60: Hes 6C **32**
Gayton La. CH60: Hes 5D **32**

Gayton Mill Cl.—Greenfields Av.

Gayton Mill Cl.
CH60: Hes 4D 32
Gayton Parkway CH60: Hes . . .6E 33
Gayton Rd. CH60: Hes 5B 32
Gaytree Ct. CH43: Bid 6A 12
Gaywood Cl. CH43: Bid 6A 12
Gelling St. L8: Liv 2G 23
Gem St. L5: Liv 6E 7
Geneva Rd. CH44: Wall 3H 13
George Rd. CH47: Hoy 1E 17
George's Dock Gates
L3: Liv 3D 14
Georges Dockway L3: Liv 4D 14
George St. CH41: Birk 6A 14
CH65: Ell P 2G 43
L3: Liv 3E 15
Georgia Av. CH62: Brom 6C 30
Geraint St. L8: Liv 1H 23
Gerald Rd. CH43: O'ton 3E 21
Gerard Av. CH45: Wall 4E 5
Gerard Rd. CH45: Wall 5D 4
CH48: W Kir 4D 16
Gerard St. L3: Liv 2F 15
Gerrard Av. CH66: Gt Sut 3C 48
Gertrude St. CH41: Birk 1B 22
Gibbs Ct. CH61: Irby 3C 26
Gibraltar Row L3: Liv 3D 14
Gibson Cl. CH61: Pens 6B 26
Gibson Ct. CH65: Ell P 1G 43
Gibson Rd. L8: Liv 6H 15
Gilbert Cl. CH63: Spit 1F 35
Gilbert St. L1: Liv 5F 15
Gildarts Gdns. L3: Liv 1E 15
Gildart St. L3: Liv 3G 15
Gillbrook Sq. *CH41: Birk 5D 12*
(off Vaughan St., not continuous)
Gills La.
CH61: Barn, Pens 5C 26
Gill St. L3: Liv 3G 15
Gilman St. L4: Walt 4H 7
Gilmartin Gro. L6: Liv 2H 15
Gilmour Mt. CH43: O'ton 3F 21
Gilroy Rd. CH48: W Kir 4E 17
Gilwell Av. CH46: More 6E 11
Gilwell Cl. CH46: More 6E 11
Ginnel, The CH62: Port S 4H 29
Girton Av. L20: Boot 1G 7
Girton Cl. CH65: Ell P 3B 50
Girton Rd. CH65: Ell P 3B 50
Girtrell Cl. CH49: Upton 2D 18
Girtrell Rd. CH49: Upton 2D 18
Girvan Dr. CH64: Lit N 1D 44
Glade, The CH47: Meols 4F 9
Glade Dr. CH66: Lit Sut 1H 47
Gladstone Cl. CH41: Birk 1G 21
Gladstone Ct. *L8: Liv 6H 15*
(off Up. Parliament St.)
Gladstone Hall Rd.
CH62: Port S 4H 29
Gladstone Rd. CH44: Wall 2H 13
CH64: Nest 5C 38
Gladstone St. L3: Liv 2E 15
Gladstone Ter. *CH64: Will 5B 40*
(off Neston Rd.)
Gladstone Theatre 5H 29
Glaisher St. L5: Liv 5H 7
Glasgow St. CH42: R Ferr 5B 22
Glasier Rd. CH46: More 4C 10
Gleaston Cl. CH62: Brom 2B 36
Gleave Cres. L6: Liv 1H 15
Glebe Hey Rd.
CH49: W'chu 4G 19
Glebelands Rd.
CH46: More 5E 11
Glebe Rd. CH45: Wall 5E 5
Glebeway Way
CH65: Ell P 2D 50
Gleggside CH48: W Kir 5E 17
Glegg St. L3: Liv 1D 14
Glen, The CH63: Spit 6A 30
Glenalmond Rd.
CH44: Wall 1H 13
Glenathol Rd.
CH66: Gt Sut 3C 48
Glenavon Rd. CH43: Pren 6E 21
Glenburn Av. CH62: East 1G 41
Glenburn Rd. CH44: Wall 2H 13
Glencoe Rd. CH45: Wall 5F 5
CH66: Gt Sut 3C 48
Glendale Cl. L8: Liv 4H 23
Glendale Gro. CH63: Spit 1H 35
Glendower St. L20: Kirk 2E 7
Glendyke Rd.
CH66: Gt Sut 3C 48
Gleneagles Cl.
CH61: Pens 6B 26
Gleneagles Rd.
CH66: Gt Sut 2C 48
Glenesk Rd. CH66: Gt Sut 3C 48
Glenfield Cl. CH43: Bid 5A 12
CH46: More 4B 10
Glenham Cl. CH47: Meols 5G 9
Glenmarsh Cl.
CH63: High B 4D 28
Glenmaye Rd.
CH66: Gt Sut 3C 48
Glenmore Rd.
CH43: O'ton 3E 21
Glen Pk. Rd. CH45: Wall 4E 5
Glen Rd. CH66: Gt Sut 2C 48
Glen Ronald Dr.
CH49: Grea 2D 18
Glenton Pk. CH64: Lit N 1D 44
Glentree Cl. CH49: Grea 2D 18
Glenwood Cl.
CH66: Lit Sut 1C 48
Glenwood Dr. CH61: Irby 2A 26
Glenwood Gdns.
CH66: Lit Sut 1C 48
Glenwood Rd.
CH66: Lit Sut 1C 48
Globe St. L4: Walt 4G 7
Gloucester Cl.
CH66: Gt Sut 6A 48
Gloucester Rd. CH45: Wall 5C 4
Gloucester St. L1: Liv 3F 15
Glover St. CH42: Tran 3G 21
L8: Liv 1F 23
Glyn Av. CH62: Brom 4C 36
Glyn Rd. CH44: Wall 6F 5
Golden Gro. L4: Walt 2H 7
Goldie St. L4: Walt 4H 7
Goldsmith Rd.
CH43: Pren 6D 20
Goldsmith Way
CH43: Pren 6D 20
Golf Links Rd. CH42: Tran 6F 21
Gonville Rd. L20: Boot 1F 7
Goodakers Ct.
CH49: W'chu 5G 19
(off Goodakers Mdw.)
Goodakers Mdw.
CH49: W'chu 5G 19
Goodall Pl. L4: Kirk 2G 7
Goodall St. L4: Kirk 2G 7
Goodison Av. L4: Walt 3H 7
Goodison Pk. 2H 7
Goodison Pl. L4: Walt 2H 7
Goodison Rd. L4: Walt 2H 7
Goodwood Dr. CH46: Leas 2F 11
Goodwood Gro.
CH66: Gt Sut 4D 48
Goodwood St. L5: Liv 6F 7
Goose Grn., The
CH47: Meols 4F 9
Goostrey Cl. CH63: Spit 2H 35
Gordon Av. CH49: Grea 4E 19
CH62: Brom 4C 36
Gordon Ct. CH49: Grea 4E 19
Gordon Rd. CH45: New B 4F 5
Gordon St. CH41: Birk 1G 21
Gordon Ter. *CH64: Will 5B 40*
(off Neston Rd.)
Goree L2: Liv 4D 14
Gore St. L8: Liv 1G 23
Gorsebank St. CH44: Wall 2G 13
Gorse Cres. CH44: Wall 3G 13
Gorsedale Pk. CH44: Wall 3H 13
Gorsedale Rd. CH44: Wall 3F 13
Gorsefield Av.
CH62: Brom 6B 36
Gorsefield Cl.
CH62: Brom 6B 36
Gorsefield Rd.
CH42: Tran 4G 21
Gorsehill Rd. CH45: New B 4E 5
CH60: Hes 2C 32
Gorse La. CH48: W Kir 6G 17
Gorse Rd. CH47: Meols 5F 9
Gorsey La. CH44: Wall 2F 13
Gorseyville Cres.
CH63: High B 4E 29
Gorseyville Rd.
CH63: High B 4E 29
Gorstons La. CH64: Lit N 1E 45
Gorst St. L4: Walt 4H 7
Goschen St. L5: Liv 4H 7
Gosford St. L8: Liv 3H 23
Gotham Rd. CH63: Spit 1G 35
Gothic St. CH42: R Ferr 5B 22
Gourleys La. CH48: W Kir 6F 17
Government Rd.
CH47: Hoy 6D 8
Gower St. L3: Liv 5E 15
Gowy Ct. CH66: Ell P 5E 43
Grace Cl. CH45: Wall 6F 5
Grace Rd. CH65: Ell P 1H 49
Grace St. L8: Liv 3H 23
Gradwell St. L1: Liv 4F 15
Grafton Cres. L8: Liv 1F 23
Grafton Dr. CH49: Upton 3H 19
Grafton Gro. L8: Liv 3G 23
Grafton Rd. CH45: New B 4F 5
CH65: Ell P 2G 43
Grafton St. CH43: O'ton 2F 21
L8: Liv 4H 23
(Beresford Rd.)
L8: Liv 1F 23
(Grafton Cres.)
L8: Liv 2G 23
(Park St.)
L8: Liv 1F 23
(Parliament St.)
Grafton Wlk. CH48: W Kir 5E 17
Graham Av. CH66: Gt Sut 2D 48
Graham Rd. CH48: W Kir 4C 16
Grainger Av. CH43: Pren 5D 20
CH48: W Kir 3D 16
Grain Ind. Est. L8: Liv 3G 23
Grain St. L8: Liv 3G 23
Grammar School La.
CH48: W Kir 6F 17
Grampian Av. CH46: More 5F 11
Grampian Way
CH46: More 5E 11
CH62: East 6C 36
CH64: Lit N 2C 44
Granary Way L3: Liv 1F 23
GRANBY 5H 15
Granby Cres. CH63: Spit 1G 35
Grand Central *L3: Liv 4G 15*
(off Hilbre St.)
GRANGE 5F 17
Grange, The CH44: Wall 1G 13
Grange Av. CH45: Wall 5F 5
Grange Ct. CH43: O'ton 4E 21
Grange Cres. CH66: Hoot 4A 42
Grange Cross Cl.
CH48: W Kir 6G 17
Grange Cross Hey
CH48: W Kir 6G 17
Grange Cross La.
CH48: W Kir 6G 17
Grange Dr. CH60: Hes 2C 32
CH63: Thorn H 4A 34
Grange Farm Cres.
CH48: W Kir 4G 17
Grange Mt. CH43: O'ton 2G 21
CH48: W Kir 5F 17
CH60: Hes 2B 32
Grange Old Rd.
CH48: W Kir 5E 17
Grange Pl. CH41: Birk 1G 21
Grange Pct. CH41: Birk 1H 21
Grange Rd. CH41: Birk 1H 21
(not continuous)
CH48: W Kir 5C 16
CH60: Hes 1B 32
CH65: Ell P 2A 50
Grange Rd. E. CH41: Birk 1A 22
Grange Road Sports Cen. . . .1F 21
Grange Rd. W.
CH41: Birk 1G 21
CH43: O'ton 1F 21
Grange Va. CH42: R Ferr 6C 22
Grange Vw. CH43: O'ton 2G 21
Grange Wlk. CH48: W Kir 6F 17
Grantham Cl. CH61: Pens 5A 26
Granton Rd. L5: Liv 5H 7
Grant Rd. CH46: Leas 1H 11
Granville Cl. CH45: Wall 5C 4
Granville Ct. CH45: Wall 5C 4
Granville Dr.
CH66: Lit Sut 6B 42
Grappenhall Rd.
CH65: Gt Sut 3F 49
Grappenhall Way
CH43: Bid 6A 12
Grasmere Av. CH43: Noct 2A 20
Grasmere Ct. *CH41: Birk 2G 21*
(off Penrith St.)
Grasmere Dr. CH45: Wall 5E 5
Grasmere Rd. CH64: Nest 1C 44
CH65: Ell P 5A 50
Grassmoor Cl.
CH62: Brom 3C 36
Grasswood Rd.
CH49: W'chu 5H 19
Grasville Rd. CH42: Tran 4A 22
Gratrix Rd. CH62: Brom 3B 36
Graylands Rd.
CH62: Port S 3A 30
Grayson St. L1: Liv 5E 15
GREASBY 4D 18
Greasby Dr. CH66: Gt Sut 3E 49
Greasby Hill Rd.
CH48: W Kir 6E 17
Greasby Rd. CH44: Wall 1E 13
CH49: Grea 4C 18
Gt. Charlotte St. L1: Liv 4F 15
(not continuous)
Gt. Crosshall St.
L3: Liv 3E 15
Gt. George Pl. L1: Liv 6G 15
Gt. George Sq. L1: Liv 5F 15
Gt. George St. L1: Liv 6G 15
Gt. Homer St. L5: Liv 5F 7
Gt. Homer St. Shop. Cen.
L5: Liv 6G 7
Gt. Howard St. L3: Liv 2D 14
L5: Liv 2D 14
GREAT MEOLS 4G 9
Gt. Mersey St. L5: Kirk 5E 7
(not continuous)
Gt. Nelson St. L3: Liv 1F 15
Gt. Newton St. L3: Liv 3H 15
Gt. Orford St. L3: Liv 4H 15
Gt. Richmond St. L3: Liv 2F 15
GREAT SUTTON 3D 48
Gt. Western Ho.
CH41: Birk 6B 14
Greaves St. L8: Liv 2H 23
Grecian Ter. L5: Liv 5G 7
Greek St. L3: Liv 3G 15
Green, The CH48: Caldy 2B 24
CH62: Brom 4B 30
CH63: Raby 1G 39
CH64: Lit N 1D 44
CH64: Nest 5B 38
Green, The CH64: Will 5B 40
CH65: Whit 5H 49
Greenacre Dr.
CH63: Brom 4A 36
Greenacres Cl. CH43: Bid 5A 12
Greenacres Ct. CH43: Bid 5A 12
Green Acres Est.
CH49: Grea 5C 18
Green Av. CH45: New B 3F 5
Green Bank CH63: Brim 1A 34
Greenbank Av.
CH45: New B 4F 5
CH66: Lit Sut 6C 42
Greenbank Dr. CH61: Pens . . .6C 26
Greenbank Rd.
CH42: Tran 4G 21
CH48: W Kir 3D 16
Greencroft Rd.
CH44: Wall 2G 13
Greendale Rd.
CH62: Port S 3G 29
Greenfield La. CH60: Hes 1H 31
Greenfield Rd.
CH66: Lit Sut 6B 42
GREENFIELDS 5A 12
Greenfields Av.
CH62: Brom 4A 36

Hornby Rd.—Kingsley Av.

Hornby Rd. CH62: Brom 2A 36
Hornby St. CH41: Birk 1B 22
Hornby Wlk. L5: Liv 1E 15
Hornet Cl. L6: Liv 6H 7
Horseman Pl. CH44: Wall 3A 14
Horsfall Gro. L8: Liv 3G 23
Horsfall St. L8: Liv 3G 23
Horstone Cres.
CH66: Gt Sut 5F 49
Horstone Gdns.
CH66: Gt Sut 5G 49
Horstone Rd. CH66: Gt Sut . . .5F 49
Hoscote Pk. CH48: W Kir 5C 16
Hose Side Rd. CH45: Wall 4E 5
Hospital Rd. CH62: Port S . . .3H 29
Hotham St. L3: Liv 3G 15
Hothfield Rd. CH44: Wall 2H 13
Hotspur St. L20: Kirk 2E 7
Houghton La. L1: Liv 4F 15
Houghton Rd.
CH49: W'chu 3H 19
Houghton St. L1: Liv 4F 15
Houghton Way *L1: Liv 4F 15*
(off St Johns Cen.)
Houlgrave Rd. L5: Liv 6E 7
Hourd Way CH66: Gt Sut 6A 48
Howard Av. CH62: Brom 3B 36
Howard Ct. CH64: Nest 4D 38
Howards Rd. CH61: Thing 3D 26
Howards Way CH64: Lit N 1E 45
Howbeck Cl. CH43: C'ton 1D 20
Howbeck Ct. CH43: O'ton 2D 20
Howbeck Dr. CH43: C'ton 1D 20
Howbeck Rd. CH43: O'ton 2D 20
Howell Dr. CH49: Grea 5D 18
Howell Rd. CH62: New F 2G 29
Howells Av. CH66: Gt Sut 4C 48
Howe St. L20: Boot 2D 6
Howgill Cl. CH66: Lit Sut 1H 47
Howson St. CH42: R Ferr 5B 22
Hoyer Ind. Est. CH65: Ell P . . .3D 50
HOYLAKE 6D 8
Hoylake Rd. CH41: Birk 3B 12
CH46: More 6B 10
Hoylake Station (Rail) 1D 16
Hoyle Rd. CH47: Hoy 5D 8
Huddleston Cl.
CH49: W'chu 4A 20
Hudson Rd. CH46: Leas 1G 11
Hughes La. CH43: O'ton 4F 21
Hughson St. L8: Liv 2G 23
Hulmewood CH63: Beb 2G 29
Humber Cl. L4: Kirk 3G 7
Humber Rd. CH66: Gt Sut 5F 49
Humber St. CH41: Birk 4D 12
Hume Ct. CH47: Meols 5E 9
Hunstanton Cl.
CH49: Upton 6G 11
Hunter St. L3: Liv 3F 15
Hunters Way CH64: Park 5A 38
Huntingdon Cl. CH46: More . . .5B 10
Hurford Av. CH65: Gt Sut 3F 49
Hurrell Rd. CH41: Birk 4B 12
Hurst Bank CH42: R Ferr 1F 29
Hurst St. L1: Liv 5E 15
Huskisson St. L8: Liv 6H 15
Huxley Cl. CH46: More 5B 10
Huxley Ct. CH66: Ell P 5F 43
Hyacinth Gro. CH46: More . . .3G 11
Hyde Cl. CH65: Gt Sut 3F 49
Hydro Av. CH48: W Kir 6D 16
Hylton Av. CH44: Wall 1E 13
Hylton Ct. CH65: Ell P 5C 50
Hyslop St. L8: Liv 1G 23

I

Iffley Cl. CH49: Upton 2D 18
Ikin Cl. CH43: Bid 4A 12
Ilchester Rd. CH41: Birk 4D 12
CH44: Wall 2H 13
Ilford Av. CH44: Wall 2F 13
Ilford St. L3: Liv 3G 15
Iliad St. L5: Liv 1G 15
Ilsley Cl. CH49: Upton 3F 19
Imison St. L9: Walt 1G 7
Imison Way L9: Walt 1G 7
Imperial Av. CH45: Wall 5G 5
Imperial Chambers *L1: Liv . . .3E 15*
(off Dale St.)
Imperial Ct. *L2: Liv 3E 15*
(off Exchange St. E.)
Imperial M. CH65: Ell P 1H 49
Imrie St. L4: Walt 1H 7
Ince Av. CH62: East 2G 41
Ince Cl. CH43: O'ton 3D 20
Ince Gro. CH43: O'ton 4D 20
Inchcape Rd. CH45: Wall 6B 4
Index St. L4: Walt 2H 7
Indigo Rd. CH65: Ell P 2D 50
Ingestre Rd. CH43: O'ton 4E 21
Ingleborough Rd.
CH42: Tran 5H 21
Ingleby Rd. CH44: Wall 2E 13
CH62: New F 1H 29
Inglegreen CH60: Hes 3D 32
Inglemere Rd. CH42: R Ferr . . .5A 22
Ingleton Cl. CH49: Grea 3D 18
Inglewood CH46: More 6D 10
Inglewood Av. CH46: More . . .6D 10
Inley Cl. CH63: Spit 1G 35
Inley Rd. CH63: Spit 1F 35
Inman Rd. CH49: Upton 1E 19
Innisfree Cl. CH66: Gt Sut 2C 48
Intake Cl. CH64: Will 5C 40
Inveresk Ct. CH43: Noct 1C 20
Inward Way CH65: Ell P 6H 43
Ionic St. CH42: R Ferr 5B 22
IRBY 4H 25
Irby Av. CH44: Wall 1E 13
Irby Cl. CH66: Gt Sut 3E 49
IRBY HEATH 3G 25
IRBY HILL 1G 25
Irby Rd. CH61: Irby 4H 25
Irbyside Rd. CH48: Frank 6B 18
Ireton St. L4: Walt 1H 7
Iris Av. CH41: Birk 5D 12
Irlam Ho. L20: Boot 1D 6
Irlam Rd. L20: Boot 1D 6
Ironbridge Vw. L8: Liv 3G 23
Irvine Rd. CH42: Tran 5H 21
Irvine Ter. CH62: New F 1H 29
Irwell Chambers *L3: Liv 3D 14*
(off Union St.)
Irwell St. L3: Liv 4D 14
Isaac St. L8: Liv 3H 23
Islay Cl. CH65: Ell P 6A 50
Islington L3: Liv 3G 15
Islington Sq. L3: Liv 2H 15
Islip Cl. CH61: Irby 2H 25
Ismay Dr. CH44: Wall 6H 5
Ismay St. L4: Walt 2H 7
Ivor Rd. CH44: Wall 6G 5
Ivy Av. CH63: High B 4E 29
Ivydale Rd. CH42: Tran 4A 22
Ivy Farm Dr. CH64: Lit N 1D 44
Ivy La. CH46: More 3E 11
Ivy St. CH41: Birk 1B 22

J

Jack McBain Ct. L3: Liv 1E 15
Jackson Cl. CH63: High B 1F 29
Jackson St. CH41: Birk 2A 22
Jacob St. L8: Liv 3H 23
Jamaica St. L1: Liv 6F 15
James Av. CH66: Gt Sut 4C 48
Jamesbrook Cl. CH41: Birk . . .5E 13
James Clarke St. L5: Liv 1E 15
James Dunne Av. L3: Liv 6E 7
James Hopkins Way L4: Kirk . . .4F 7
James Larkin Way L4: Kirk 4F 7
James St. CH43: O'ton 3G 21
CH44: Wall 3A 14
L2: Liv 4E 15
James Street Station (Rail)
. . . . .4E 15
Jarrow Cl. CH43: O'ton 3F 21
Jasmine Cl. CH49: Upton 6D 10
L5: Liv 6H 7
Jasmine M. L17: Aig 4H 23
Jason St. L5: Liv 5G 7
Jason Wlk. L5: Liv 5G 7
Jedburgh Av. CH66: Lit Sut . . .2H 47
Jeffreys Dr. CH49: Grea 2D 18
Jellicoe Cl. CH48: Caldy 3B 24
Jenkinson St. L3: Liv 2G 15
Jenner Dr. CH46: Leas 3G 11
Jersey Av. CH65: Ell P 6A 50
Jessamine Rd. CH42: Tran . . .4A 22
Jessica Ho. L20: Kirk 2F 7
Joan Av. CH46: More 5D 10
CH49: Grea 3E 19
Jocelyn Cl. CH63: Spit 6G 29
John Bagot Cl. L5: Liv 6G 7
John F Kennedy Hgts.
L3: Liv 1G 15
John Moores Cl. L7: Liv 5H 15
John Moores University
Avril Robarts Cen. 3E 15
Byrom St. 2F 15
Henry Cotton Campus, The
. . . . .3F 15
(off Trueman St.)
John Nicholas Cres.
CH65: Ell P 1A 50
Johnson Rd. CH43: Pren 6D 20
Johnson St. L3: Liv 2E 15
John St. CH41: Birk 6B 14
CH65: Ell P 1H 49
L3: Liv 2G 15
John Willis Ho.
CH42: R Ferr 5C 22
John Yeoman Cl.
CH64: Lit N 6D 38
Jones St. L3: Liv 4G 15
Jonson Rd. CH64: Nest 4C 38
Jordan St. L1: Liv 6F 15
Joseph Groome Towers
CH65: Ell P 1A 50
Josephine Butler Sq.
L3: Liv 2H 15
Joshua Cl. L5: Liv 5G 7
Jubilee Cres. CH62: Port S . . .4H 29
Jubilee Dr. CH48: W Kir 3D 16
Jubilee Grn. CH65: Ell P 3A 50
Juliet Av. CH63: High B 2E 29
Juliet Gdns. CH63: High B 2E 29
Junc. Eight Bus. Cen.
CH65: Ell P 1G 49
Junc. One Retail Pk.
CH44: Wall 2B 12
June Av. CH62: Brom 3C 36
Juniper Cl. CH49: Grea 5C 18
Juniper Dr. CH66: Gt Sut 6E 49
Juniper Gro. CH66: Gt Sut 6F 49
Juniper St. L20: Kirk 3E 7
Juvenal Pl. L3: Liv 1G 15
Juvenal St. L3: Liv 1F 15

K

Kale Cl. CH48: W Kir 6D 16
Karen Way CH66: Gt Sut 4D 48
Karslake Rd. CH44: Wall 2H 13
Kearsley Cl. L4: Kirk 4G 7
Kearsley St. L4: Walt 4G 7
Keats Cl. CH66: Gt Sut 6A 48
Keble Dr. CH45: Wall 5B 4
Keble Rd. L20: Boot 2E 7
Keegan Dr. CH44: Wall 3A 14
Keele Cl. CH43: Bid 3A 12
Keel Hey CH64: Will 4D 40
Keepers La. CH63: Store 4B 28
Keighley Av. CH45: Wall 6C 4
Keightley St. CH41: Birk 6G 13
Keith Av. L4: Walt 2H 7
Keith Dr. CH63: East 6A 36
Kellet's Pl. CH42: R Ferr 4B 22
Kellett Rd. CH46: Leas 2H 11
Kelmscott Cl. CH66: Gt Sut . . .5D 48
Kelmscott Dr. CH44: Wall 1C 12
Kelsall Av. CH62: East 2G 41
Kelsall Cl. CH43: O'ton 4D 20
CH62: East 2G 41
Kelvin Ct. CH44: Wall 3A 14
Kelvin Pk. CH41: Birk 4H 13
Kelvin Rd. CH41: Tran 3A 22
CH44: Wall 4A 14
Kelvinside CH44: Wall 4H 13
Kemlyn Rd. L4: Walt 4H 7
Kempson Ter. CH63: Beb 5F 29
Kempston St. L3: Liv 3G 15
Kempton Rd. CH62: New F . . .1H 29
Kendal Cl. CH63: Beb 3F 29
CH66: Gt Sut 5D 48
Kendal Dr. CH66: Gt Sut 5D 48
Kendal Rd. CH44: Wall 3E 13
Kendal St. CH41: Birk 1A 22
Kenilworth Ct. CH65: Ell P 4C 50
(not continuous)
Kenilworth Dr. CH61: Pens . . .4B 26
Kenilworth Gdns.
CH49: Upton 1E 19
Kenilworth Rd. CH44: Wall . . .2H 13
CH64: Nest 1C 44
Kenmore Rd. CH43: Pren 6C 20
Kennet Rd. CH63: High B 4D 28
Kensington L7: Liv 3H 15
Kensington Gdns.
CH46: More 5F 11
Kensington Rd. CH65: Ell P . . .2G 49
Kent Cl. CH63: Brom 3H 35
Kentmere Dr. CH61: Pens 6B 26
Kent M. CH43: O'ton 3E 21
Kent Pl. CH41: Birk 1H 21
Kentridge Dr. CH66: Gt Sut . . .4D 48
Kent Rd. CH44: Wall 2E 13
Kent St. CH43: O'ton 3E 21
L1: Liv 5F 15
(not continuous)
Kenwick Cl. CH66: Gt Sut 4C 48
Kenwyn Rd. CH45: Wall 6F 5
Kenyon Ct. *L8: Liv 1H 23*
(off Park Rd.)
Kenyon Ter. CH43: O'ton 2F 21
Keppel St. L20: Boot 2D 6
Kerry Cft. CH66: Gt Sut 6E 49
Kestrel Av. CH49: Upton 1D 18
Kestrel Cl. CH49: Upton 1D 18
Kestrel Rd. CH46: More 5C 10
CH60: Hes 4E 33
Keswick Av. CH63: East 1E 41
Keswick Gdns. CH63: Brom . . .6A 36
Keswick Pl. CH43: Bid 4B 12
Keswick Rd. CH45: Wall 4D 4
Kevelioc Cl. CH63: Spit 6F 29
Kew St. L5: Liv 6F 7
Kiddman St. L9: Walt 1H 7
Kilburn Av. CH62: East 5C 36
Killarney Gro. CH44: Wall 2E 13
Killington Way L4: Kirk 3G 7
Kilmalcolm Cl. CH43: O'ton . . .3D 20
Kiln Rd. CH49: W'chu 4G 19
Kimberley Cl. L8: Liv 6H 15
Kimberley Rd. CH45: Wall 5F 5
Kindale Rd. CH43: Pren 6C 20
Kinder St. L6: Liv 2H 15
King Edward Dr.
CH62: Port S 3H 29
King Edward Ind. Est.
L3: Liv 2D 14
(off Gibraltar Row)
King Edward Pde. L3: Liv 3D 14
King Edward St. L3: Liv 3D 14
Kingfisher Way
CH49: Upton 1D 18
King George Dr. CH44: Wall . . .5G 5
King George's Dr.
CH62: Port S 3H 29
King George's Way
CH43: Bid 6C 12
Kinglake Rd. CH44: Wall 6H 5
Kinglass Rd. CH63: Spit 6H 29
King's Av. CH47: Meols 5F 9
Kingsbrook Way
CH63: High B 1D 28
King's Brow CH63: High B 3D 28
Kingsbury CH48: W Kir 5F 17
Kings Cl. CH63: High B 2D 28
Kings Ct. CH47: Hoy 6C 8
CH63: High B 3D 28
Kingsdale Av. CH42: Tran 5H 21
Kings Dock St. L1: Liv 6F 15
Kingsdown St. CH41: Tran 3A 22
King's Dr. CH48: Caldy 2A 24
CH61: Pens 4B 26
King's Dr. Nth.
CH48: W Kir 6G 17
King's Gap, The CH47: Hoy 6C 8
Kingsland Rd. CH42: Tran 3G 21
King's La. CH63: High B 2D 28
Kingsley Av. CH62: East 2G 41

Kingsley Cl.—Lichfield Dr.

Kingsley Cl. CH61: Pens 6C **26**
Kingsley Rd. CH44: Wall 2F **13**
CH65: Ell P 2A **50**
Kingsley St. CH41: Birk 5E **13**
Kingsmead Gro.
CH43: O'ton 2D **20**
Kingsmead Rd.
CH43: O'ton 2D **20**
CH46: More 3F **11**
Kingsmead Rd. Nth.
CH43: O'ton 2D **20**
Kingsmead Rd. Sth.
CH43: O'ton 2D **20**
Kings M. CH66: Lit Sut 6C **42**
Kings Mt. CH43: O'ton 3F **21**
Kings Pde.
CH45: Wall, New B 3B **4**
L3: Liv 5E **15**
Kings Rd. CH63: High B 1D **28**
CH66: Lit Sut 6C **42**
L20: Boot 1E **7**
Kings Sq. CH41: Birk 1A **22**
Kings Ter. L20: Boot 2E **7**
Kingston Cl. CH46: More 5E **11**
King St. CH42: R Ferr 6C **22**
CH44: Wall 6H **5**
CH65: Ell P 1A **50**
Kingsville Rd.
CH63: High B 4E **29**
Kings Wlk. CH42: R Ferr 6C **22**
CH48: W Kir 5E **17**
Kingsway CH44: Wall 2B **14**
CH45: Wall 5E **5**
CH60: Hes 5E **33**
CH63: High B 2D **28**
L3: Liv 2E **15**
Kingsway Ct. *L1: Liv 6G 15*
(off Raffles St.)
L3: Liv 1F **15**
Kingsway Pk. L3: Liv 1F **15**
Kingsway Tunnel App.
CH44: Wall 1C **12**
Kings Wharf CH41: Birk 4A **14**
Kingswood Blvd.
CH63: High B 1E **29**
Kingswood Rd. CH44: Wall 6G **5**
Kington Rd. CH48: W Kir 4C **16**
Kinloss Rd. CH49: Grea 4C **18**
Kinmel Cl. CH41: Birk 6H **13**
Kinmel St. L8: Liv 2H **23**
Kinnaird Rd. CH45: Wall 5E **5**
Kinnerley Rd. CH65: Whit 4G **49**
Kinnerton Cl. CH46: More 5B **10**
Kinnington Way CH1: Back . . .6A **48**
Kinross Rd. CH45: Wall 5B **4**
Kinsey Rd. CH65: Ell P 6B **50**
Kintore Cl. CH63: East 1E **41**
Kintyre Cl. CH65: Ell P 6A **50**
Kipling Av. CH42: R Ferr 6B **22**
Kirby Cl. CH48: W Kir 6E **17**
Kirby Mt. CH48: W Kir 1A **24**
Kirby Pk. CH48: W Kir 6E **17**
Kirby Pk. Mans.
CH48: W Kir 6D **16**
Kirkburn Cl. L8: Liv 3H **23**
Kirk Cotts. CH45: Wall 4F **5**
KIRKDALE **3G 7**
Kirkdale Rd. L5: Kirk 5F **7**
Kirkdale Station (Rail) **2F 7**
Kirkdale Va. L4: Walt 4G **7**
Kirket Cl. CH63: Beb 5G **29**
Kirket La. CH63: Beb 5F **29**
Kirkfield Gro. CH42: R Ferr . . .6C **22**
Kirkland Av. CH42: Tran 5H **21**
Kirkland Rd. CH45: New B 3G **5**
Kirklands, The CH48: W Kir . . .6E **17**
Kirkmount CH49: Upton 2G **19**
Kirk St. L5: Liv 5G **7**
Kirkway CH45: Wall 4F **5**
CH49: Grea 3E **19**
CH49: Upton 2F **19**
CH63: High B 2D **28**
Kitchen St. L1: Liv 6F **15**
Knap, The CH60: Hes 5C **32**
Knaresborough Rd.
CH44: Wall 1D **12**
Knightsbridge Ct.
CH43: Noct 4B **20**
Knight St. L1: Liv 5G **15**
Knoll, The CH43: O'ton 4E **21**
Knottingley Dr.
CH66: Gt Sut 2C **48**
Knowe, The CH64: Will 5C **40**
Knowle Cl. CH66: Gt Sut 4E **49**
Knowles St. CH41: Birk 6G **13**
Knowsley Cl. CH42: R Ferr . . .6C **22**
Knowsley Ct. CH42: R Ferr . . .6C **22**
Knowsley Rd. CH42: R Ferr . . .6C **22**
CH45: Wall 5E **5**
Knowsley St. L4: Walt 1H **7**
Knox Cl. CH62: Port S 3H **29**
Knox St. CH41: Birk 1B **22**
Knutsford Grn. CH46: More . . .4F **11**
Knutsford Rd. CH46: More 4E **11**
Kronsbec Av. CH66: Lit Sut . . .1D **48**
Kylemore Cl. CH61: Pens 6A **26**
Kylemore Dr. CH61: Pens 6A **26**
Kylemore Rd. CH43: O'ton . . .3E **21**
Kylemore Way CH61: Pens . . .6A **26**

L

Laburnum Ct. *L8: Liv 3H 23*
(off Weller Way)
Laburnum Farm Cl.
CH64: Ness 2E **45**
Laburnum Gro. CH61: Irby . . .3H **25**
CH66: Whit 6B **48**
Laburnum Rd. CH43: O'ton . . .3F **21**
CH45: New B 4F **5**
Lace St. L3: Liv 2F **15**
Ladies Wlk. CH64: Nest 5C **38**
Lad La. L3: Liv 3D **14**
Ladybower Cl.
CH49: Upton 1E **19**
Lady Chapel Cl. L1: Liv 6G **15**
Ladyewood Rd. CH44: Wall . . .2G **13**
Ladyfield CH43: Bid 6A **12**
Lady Lever Art Gallery **3H 29**
Lagan Ho. CH46: Leas 1E **11**
Laird Cl. CH41: Birk 5D **12**
Lairdside Technical Pk.
CH41: Tran 3B **22**
Lairds Pl. L3: Liv 1F **15**
Laird St. CH41: Birk 5D **12**
Lake Ent. Pk. CH62: Brom 1C **36**
Lakeland Cl. L1: Liv 5F **15**
Lake Pl. CH47: Hoy 6D **8**
Lake Rd. CH47: Hoy 6D **8**
Lakeside Ct. CH45: New B 3G **5**
Lake St. L4: Walt 4H **7**
Lambert St. L3: Liv 3G **15**
(Kempston St.)
L3: Liv 3G 15
(off Lambert Way)
Lambert Way L3: Liv 3G **15**
Lambeth Rd. L4: Kirk 4F **7**
L5: Kirk 4F **7**
Lambeth Wlk. L4: Kirk 4F **7**
Lambourne Cl.
CH66: Gt Sut 6A **48**
Lambrigg Row L5: Liv 4H **7**
Lamport St. L8: Liv 1G **23**
Lancaster Av. CH45: Wall 6F **5**
Lancaster Cl. CH62: Port S . . .3H **29**
L5: Kirk 5F **7**
Lancaster Gdns.
CH65: Ell P 4B **50**
Lancaster St. L5: Kirk 5F **7**
Lancaster Wlk. L5: Kirk 5F **7**
Lance Cl. L5: Liv 6H **7**
Lancelots Hey L3: Liv 3D **14**
Lancelyn Ct. CH63: Spit 6G **29**
Lancelyn Pct. *CH63: Spit 6G 29*
(off Spital Rd.)
Lancelyn Ter. CH63: Beb 5F **29**
Lancers Cft. CH66: Gt Sut 6E **49**
Lancing Rd. CH65: Ell P 3B **50**
LANDICAN **1E 27**
Landican Cemetery & Crematorium
CH49: W'chu 1D **26**
Landican La. CH49: W'chu . . .6A **20**
CH63: Store 3H **27**
Landican Rd. CH49: W'chu . . .2D **26**
Landmark, The L5: Liv 6G **7**
Landor Cl. L5: Liv 6E **7**
Landseer Av. CH64: Lit N 6D **38**
Landseer Rd. L5: Liv 6H **7**
Langdale Av. CH61: Pens 5B **26**
Langdale Rd. CH45: Wall 4D **4**
CH63: Beb 5E **29**
Langfield Gro. CH62: Brom . . .6B **36**
Langham Ct. L4: Walt 3H **7**
Langham St. L4: Walt 3H **7**
Langham St. Ind. Est.
L4: Walt 3H **7**
Lang La. CH48: W Kir 4D **16**
Lang La. Sth. CH48: W Kir . . .5E **17**
Langley Cl. CH63: Spit 1G **35**
Langley Ct. CH65: Ell P 4C **50**
Langley Rd. CH63: Spit 1G **35**
Langley St. L8: Liv 1G **23**
Langrove St. L5: Liv 6G **7**
Langsdale St. L3: Liv 2G **15**
(not continuous)
Langstone Av. CH49: Grea 5C **18**
Langtry Cl. L4: Kirk 2F **7**
Langtry Rd. L4: Kirk 3F **7**
Lansdowne Cl. CH41: Birk 5E **13**
Lansdowne Ct. CH43: Bid 5D **12**
Lansdowne Pl. CH43: Bid 5D **12**
L5: Liv 5H **7**
Lansdowne Rd. CH41: Birk . . .5D **12**
CH43: Bid 5D **12**
CH45: Wall 4D **4**
Lanyork Rd. L3: Liv 2D **14**
Lapwing Ri. CH60: Hes 5B **32**
Lapworth Cl. CH46: More 5B **10**
Lapworth St. L5: Kirk 5F **7**
Larch Ct. *L8: Liv 3H 23*
(off Weller Way)
Larchdale Cl. CH66: Whit 6A **48**
Larch Gro. CH43: Bid 5C **12**
Larch Rd. CH42: Tran 2G **21**
Larchwood Cl. CH61: Pens . . .6B **26**
Larchwood Dr.
CH63: High B 2E **29**
Larcombe Av. CH49: Upton . . .2F **19**
Larkhill Av. CH49: Upton 6G **11**
Larkhill Way CH49: Upton 6G **11**
Larkin Cl. CH62: New F 2G **29**
Larksway CH60: Hes 3D **32**
Larton Farm Cl.
CH48: W Kir 5G **17**
Larton Rd. CH48: W Kir 4G **17**
Lartonwood CH48: W Kir 4G **17**
Latchford Rd. CH60: Hes 5D **32**
Latham St. L5: Kirk 5F **7**
(not continuous)
Latham Way CH63: Spit 1H **35**
Lathom Av. CH44: Wall 1F **13**
Latimer St. L5: Liv 5F **7**
Laund, The CH45: Wall 6D **4**
Laurel Av. CH60: Hes 2B **32**
CH63: High B 5E **29**
Laurelbanks CH60: Hes 2A **32**
Laurel Dr. CH64: Will 4D **40**
CH65: Whit 5H **49**
Laurelhurst Av. CH61: Pens . . .5C **26**
Laurel Rd. CH42: Tran 3H **21**
Laurels, The CH46: Leas 2E **11**
Laurence Deacon Ct.
CH41: Birk 6G **13**
Lavan Cl. L6: Liv 2H **15**
Lavan St. L6: Liv 2H **15**
Lavrock Bank L8: Liv 3G **23**
Lawford Dr. CH60: Hes 3E **33**
Lawns, The CH43: Bid 6B **12**
Lawns Av. CH63: Raby M 5H **35**
Lawnside Cl. CH42: R Ferr . . .6B **22**
Lawrence Ct. CH42: R Ferr . . .1G **29**
Lawton St. L1: Liv 4F **15**
Laxey St. L8: Liv 1G **23**
Laxton Cl. CH66: Gt Sut 6A **48**
Layton Av. CH43: Pren 5D **20**
Leach Way CH61: Irby 3G **25**
Lea Cl. CH43: Noct 3C **20**
Leadenhall Cl. L5: Liv 5H **7**
Leafield Cl. CH61: Irby 3B **26**
Leahurst University of Liverpool Veterinary Field Station
. . . .**6H 39**
Leamington Cl. CH64: Nest . . .1C **44**
Leamington Gdns.
CH49: W'chu 3H **19**
Leander Rd. CH45: Wall 6E **5**
Lea Rd. CH44: Wall 6G **5**
Leas, The CH45: Wall 4C **4**
CH61: Thing 3D **26**
Leas Cl. CH66: Gt Sut 2C **48**
LEASOWE **1H 11**
Leasowe Av. CH45: Wall 5C **4**
Leasowe Gdns. CH46: Leas . . .2E **11**
Leasowe Recreation Cen. **2G 11**
Leasowe Rd. CH44: Wall 2D **10**
CH45: Wall 2D **10**
CH46: Leas 2D **10**
Leasoweside CH46: Leas 1H **11**
Leasowe Station (Rail) **3F 11**
Leas Pk. CH47: Hoy 3C **16**
Leather La. L2: Liv 3E **15**
Leaway CH49: Grea 3D **18**
Leawood Gro. CH46: More . . .5F **11**
Ledbury Cl. CH43: O'ton 5C **20**
LEDSHAM **6H 47**
Ledsham Cl. CH43: Noct 3C **20**
Ledsham Ct. CH66: Lit Sut . . .1B **48**
Ledsham Hall La.
CH66: Led 2G **47**
Ledsham La. CH66: Led 3G **47**
Ledsham Pk. Dr.
CH66: Lit Sut 1A **48**
Ledsham Rd. CH66: Lit Sut . . .2H **47**
Ledsham Village
CH66: Led 6H **47**
Leece St. L1: Liv 5G **15**
Leeds St. L3: Liv 2D **14**
Lee Rd. CH47: Hoy 6E **9**
Lees Av. CH42: R Ferr 5B **22**
Lees La. CH64: Lit N, Nest . . .1E **45**
CH65: Ell P 3B **50**
Leeswood Rd.
CH49: W'chu 4G **19**
Legh Rd. CH62: New F 2H **29**
Legion La. CH62: Brom 2B **36**
Leigh Bri. Way L5: Liv 6E **7**
Leigh Pl. L1: Liv 4F **15**
Leigh Rd. CH48: W Kir 4D **16**
Leigh St. L1: Liv 4F **15**
(not continuous)
Leighton Av. CH47: Meols 5G **9**
Leighton Chase CH64: Nest . . .4B **38**
Leighton Ct. CH64: Nest 5B **38**
Leighton Pk. CH64: Nest 5B **38**
Leighton Rd. CH41: Tran 3A **22**
CH64: Nest 2A **38**
Leightons, The CH64: Nest . . .5B **38**
Leighton St. L4: Kirk 2G **7**
Leison St. L4: Kirk 4F **7**
(not continuous)
Leiston Cl. CH61: Irby 2A **26**
Lemon St. L5: Kirk 5F **7**
Lennox Av. CH45: New B 4F **5**
Lennox La. CH43: Bid 4A **12**
Lenthall St. L4: Walt 1H **7**
Leo Casino **6F 15**
Leominster Rd. CH44: Wall 1F **13**
Leonard Ho. CH41: Birk 4B **14**
Leonora St. L8: Liv 3H **23**
Leopold St. CH44: Wall 2A **14**
Leslie Av. CH49: Grea 4D **18**
Lester Cl. L4: Kirk 4G **7**
Lester Dr. CH61: Irby 2G **25**
Lestock St. L8: Liv 6G **15**
Leta St. L4: Walt 2H **7**
(not continuous)
Lethbridge Cl. L5: Kirk 5E **7**
Letitia St. L8: Liv 2H **23**
Letterstone Cl. L6: Liv 1H **15**
Letterstone Wlk. L6: Liv 1H **15**
Levens Hey CH46: More 5D **10**
Leven St. L4: Kirk 3G **7**
Leven Wlk. CH66: Ell P 5G **43**
Lever Av. CH44: Wall 3A **14**
Lever C'way.
CH63: High B, Store 4A **28**
Leverhulme Ct. CH63: Beb . . .5G **29**
Lever Ter. CH42: Tran 4A **22**
Lewis Cl. CH65: Ell P 6A **50**
Lewisham Rd.
CH62: Port S 3A **30**
Leyburn Rd. CH45: Wall 5D **4**
Liberton Ct. L5: Liv 5H **7**
Lichfield Dr.
CH66: Gt Sut 6A **48**

Millers Bri. Ind. Est.—Newington

Millers Bri. Ind. Est.
L20: Boot 1D **6**
Millers Cl. CH46: More 5B **10**
Millersdale Cl.
CH62: East 6D **36**
Millers Way CH46: More 5C **10**
Millfield CH64: Nest 4C **38**
Millfield Cl. CH63: High B 4D **28**
Millfield Ter. CH66: Lit Sut 6C **42**
Mill Grn. CH64: Will 5B **40**
Mill Hey Rd. CH48: Caldy 3B **24**
Mill Hill CH43: O'ton 4E **21**
Mill Hill Rd. CH61: Irby 1G **25**
Millhouse Cl. CH46: More 4B **10**
Millhouse La. CH46: More 4B **10**
Millington Cl. CH43: Pren 6C **20**
Mill La. CH44: Wall 2E **13**
CH49: Grea 4C **18**
CH60: Hes 3D **32**
CH64: Burt 6G **45**
CH64: Ness 2E **45**
CH64: Will 4A **40**
CH66: Ell P, Gt Sut 3D **48**
L3: Liv 3F **15**
Mill La. Ind. Est.
CH2: Lit Stan 6D **50**
Mill Pk. Dr. CH62: East 2G **41**
Mill Rd. CH61: Thing 3D **26**
CH62: Brom 6B **30**
CH63: High B 2D **28**
L6: Liv 1H **15**
(not continuous)
Mill St. CH42: Tran 3H **21**
CH64: Nest 5B **38**
L8: Liv 1G **23**
Mill Ter. CH63: High B 4D **28**
Millthwaite Ct. CH44: Wall 1D **12**
Millthwaite Rd. CH44: Wall 1D **12**
Mill Vw. L8: Liv 2G **23**
Mill Vw. Dr. CH63: High B 3C **28**
Millwood CH63: High B 3D **28**
Mill Yd. CH61: Thing 3D **26**
Milman Cl. CH49: Upton 3F **19**
Milman Rd. L4: Walt 2H **7**
Milner Cop CH60: Hes 3C **32**
Milner Rd. CH60: Hes 3C **32**
Milner St. CH41: Birk 5E **13**
Milnthorpe Cl. L4: Kirk 3G **7**
Milton Cl. CH65: Ell P 3B **50**
Milton Cres. CH60: Hes 2C **32**
Milton Grn. CH61: Thing 3D **26**
Milton Pavement
CH41: Birk 1H **21**
Milton Rd. CH42: Tran 3G **21**
CH44: Wall 3H **13**
CH48: W Kir 4C **16**
CH65: Ell P 3B **50**
L4: Walt 1G **7**
Milton Rd. E. CH42: Tran 3H **21**
Minishull St. L7: Liv 4H **15**
Minster Ct. L7: Liv 5H **15**
Miranda Av. CH63: High B 2E **29**
Miranda Pl. L20: Kirk 2F **7**
Miranda Rd. L20: Boot 1F **7**
Miriam Pl. CH41: Birk 5D **12**
Miskelly St. L20: Kirk 3E **7**
Miston St. L20: Kirk 3E **7**
Mitchell Pl. *L1: Liv 4F **15***
(off Bk. Lime St.)
Mitylene St. L5: Liv 5G **7**
Mobberley Way CH63: Spit 6G **29**
Mockbeggar Dr. CH45: Wall 4C **4**
Mockbeggar Wharf
CH45: Wall 4C **4**
Modred St. L8: Liv 2H **23**
Moira Sephton Ct.
CH43: Noct 3B **20**
Moira St. L6: Liv 3H **15**
Mollington Link CH41: Birk 2A **22**
Mollington Rd. CH44: Wall 2G **13**
Mollington St. CH41: Birk 2A **22**
Molyneux Cl. CH49: Upton 2F **19**
Molyneux Dr. CH45: New B 3F **5**
Mona St. CH41: Birk 6D **12**
Monk Rd. CH44: Wall 1F **13**
Monks Ferry CH41: Birk 1B **22**
Monks Gro. CH65: Ell P 1H **49**
Monk St. CH41: Birk 1B **22**
L5: Liv 5H **7**
Monks Way CH48: W Kir 5E **17**
CH63: Beb 5F **29**
Monmouth Rd. CH44: Wall 1D **12**
Monro Cl. L8: Liv 3H **23**
Monro St. L8: Liv 3H **23**
Montgomery Hill
CH48: Caldy, Frank 1D **24**
Montpelier Dr. L8: Liv 3H **23**
Montpellier Cres.
CH45: New B 3E **5**
Montpellier Ho.
CH45: New B 3E **5**
Montrose Av. CH44: Wall 4A **14**
Montrose Ct. CH47: Hoy 1D **16**
Monument Pl. L3: Liv 3G **15**
Moorcroft Rd. CH45: Wall 6B **4**
Moore Av. CH42: R Ferr 5A **22**
Moore's Ho. L4: Walt 1H **7**
Moorfield Dr. CH64: Park 3A **38**
Moorfields L2: Liv 3E **15**
Moorfields Av. CH43: Noct 3B **20**
Moorfields Station (Rail) **3E 15**
Moorings, The CH41: Birk 2H **21**
CH60: Hes 3G **31**
Moorings Cl. CH64: Park 4A **38**
Moorland Cl. CH60: Hes 4C **32**
Moorland Pk. CH60: Hes 4C **32**
Moorland Rd. CH42: Tran 4A **22**
CH66: Ell P 5E **43**
Moor La. CH60: Hes 3C **32**
L4: Walt 1H **7**
Moor Pl. L3: Liv 3G **15**
MOORSIDE **6A 38**
Moorside Av. CH64: Park 5A **38**
Moorside La. CH64: Park 6A **38**
Moor St. L2: Liv 4E **15**
Moorway CH60: Hes 3D **32**
Morecroft Rd. CH42: R Ferr 5C **22**
Morello Dr. CH63: Spit 1H **35**
MORETON **5E 11**
MORETON COMMON **1D 10**
Moreton Gro. CH45: Wall 5C **4**
Moreton Rd. CH49: Upton 6F **11**
Moreton Station (Rail) **3E 11**
Morland Av. CH62: Brom 5B **36**
CH64: Lit N 6D **38**
Morley Av. CH41: Birk 5F **13**
Morley Rd. CH44: Wall 2E **13**
Morley St. L4: Walt 4G **7**
Mornington Av. CH65: Ell P 2A **50**
Mornington Rd.
CH45: New B 4F **5**
Mornington St. L8: Liv 2G **23**
Morpeth Cl. CH46: More 5B **10**
Morpeth Rd. CH47: Hoy 2C **16**
Morpeth St. L8: Liv 6H **15**
Morpeth Wharf CH41: Birk 5A **14**
Morris Ct. CH43: O'ton 2D **20**
Mortar Mill Quay
CH41: Birk 4H **13**
Mortimer St. CH41: Birk 6B **14**
Morton St. L8: Liv 2H **23**
(not continuous)
Mortuary Rd. CH45: Wall 5F **5**
Morval Cres. L4: Walt 1G **7**
Mosedale Rd. CH62: Brom 1C **36**
Moseley Av. CH45: Wall 1E **13**
Moseley Rd. CH63: Spit 2G **35**
Moses St. L8: Liv 3H **23**
Moss Cl. CH64: Will 5C **40**
Mossdene Rd. CH44: Wall 1D **12**
Moss Gro. CH42: Tran 5F **21**
Mosslands Cl.
CH66: Gt Sut 5E **49**
Mosslands Dr. CH44: Wall 6C **4**
CH45: Wall 6C **4**
Moss La. CH42: Tran 5F **21**
Mossley Av. CH62: Brom 3B **36**
Mossley Rd. CH42: Tran 4A **22**
Moss St. L6: Liv 3H **15**
Moss Va. CH66: Lit Sut 5D **42**
Mossy Bank Rd.
CH44: Wall 1H **13**
Moston Way CH66: Gt Sut 4F **49**
Mostyn Av. CH48: W Kir 6D **16**
CH60: Hes 3H **31**
Mostyn Cl. L4: Kirk 4G **7**
Mostyn Gdns. CH64: Park 4A **38**
Mostyn Sq. CH64: Park 4A **38**
Mostyn St. CH44: Wall 2F **13**
Mould St. L5: Liv 5F **7**
Mounsey Rd. CH42: Tran 2H **21**
Mount, The CH44: Wall 1G **13**
CH60: Hes 3B **32**
CH63: Beb 4G **29**
Mount Av. CH60: Hes 3B **32**
CH63: High B 2D **28**
Mount Ct. CH45: New B 3E **5**
Mount Dr. CH63: High B 2D **28**
Mt. Farm Way
CH66: Gt Sut 5C **48**
Mount Gro. CH41: Birk 2G **21**
Mount Gro. Pl. CH41: Birk 2G **21**
Mt. Haven Cl. CH49: Upton 2G **19**
Mount Olive CH43: O'ton 4E **21**
Mount Pk. CH63: High B 2D **28**
Mount Pleasant
CH43: O'ton 4F **21**
L3: Liv 4G **15**
Mt. Pleasant Rd.
CH45: New B, Wall 5E **5**
Mount Rd. CH42: Tran 6G **21**
CH45: Wall 3E **5**
CH48: W Kir 6E **17**
CH49: Upton 2G **19**
CH63: High B, Spit 4C **28**
Mount St. L1: Liv 5G **15**
Mt. Vernon Rd. L7: Liv 3H **15**
Mt. Vernon St. L7: Liv 3H **15**
Mt. Vernon Vw. L7: Liv 3H **15**
Mountview Cl. L8: Liv 2H **23**
Mountway CH63: High B 2D **28**
Mt. Wood Rd. CH42: Tran 1C **28**
Mourne Cl. CH66: Lit Sut 1A **48**
Mowbray Ct. L20: Kirk 2E **7**
Mudhouse La. CH64: Burt 5A **46**
Mulberry Ct. *L7: Liv 5H **15***
(off Mulberry St.)
Mulberry Gro. CH44: Wall 2H **13**
Mulberry Pl. L7: Liv 5H **15**
Mulberry Rd. CH42: R Ferr 5B **22**
Mulberry St. L7: Liv 5H **15**
(not continuous)
Mulgrave St. L8: Liv 6H **15**
Mull Cl. CH65: Ell P 6A **50**
Mulveton Rd. CH63: Spit 6F **29**
Mumfords Gro. CH47: Meols 4G **9**
Mumfords La. CH47: Meols 4F **9**
Muncaster Cl. CH62: Brom 2B **36**
Muriel St. L4: Walt 3H **7**
MURRAYFIELD BUPA HOSPITAL
4F 27
Murrayfield Dr. CH46: Leas 1F **11**
Murray Gro. CH48: W Kir 4C **16**
Mus. of Liverpool Life 4D 14
Mynsule Rd. CH63: Spit 6F **29**
Myrtle Gro. CH44: Wall 2H **13**
Myrtle Pde. L7: Liv 5H **15**
Myrtle St. CH65: Ell P 2G **43**
L7: Liv 5H **15**

N

Naburn Gro. CH46: More 6E **11**
Nairn Cl. CH63: East 1F **41**
Nansen Gro. L4: Walt 2H **7**
Nant Pk. Ct. CH45: New B 3G **5**
Nantwich Cl. CH49: W'chu 5G **19**
Nantwich Rd. CH66: Gt Sut 4F **49**
Napier Dr. CH46: More 5F **11**
Napier Rd. CH62: New F 1H **29**
Napier St. L20: Boot 2D **6**
Naples Rd. CH44: Wall 2H **13**
Napps Way CH61: Hes 1C **32**
Naseby Cl. CH43: Noct 3A **20**
Naseby St. L4: Walt 1H **7**
Navigation Wharf L3: Liv 1F **23**
Naylor Ct. CH66: Ell P 1E **49**
Naylor Cres. CH66: Ell P 5F **43**
Naylor Rd. CH43: Bid 5C **12**
Naylor St. L3: Liv 2E **15**
Neale Dr. CH49: Grea 4E **19**
Needham Cres.
CH43: Noct 3B **20**
Needwood Dr. CH63: Beb 6F **29**
Nelson Ct. CH42: R Ferr 6C **22**
CH45: New B 2F **5**
Nelson Dr. CH61: Pens 5A **26**
Nelson Memorial *3E 15*
(off Exchange Pas. W.)
Nelson Rd. CH42: R Ferr 6C **22**
CH65: Ell P 2G **43**
Nelson's Cft. CH63: Beb 6G **29**
Nelson St. CH45: New B 4G **5**
L1: Liv 6F **15**
L20: Boot 1D **6**
Neptune St. CH41: Birk 5H **13**
Neptune Theatre 4F 15
NESS **2E 45**
Ness Acre La. CH64: Will 5A **40**
Ness Botanical Gardens 3E 45
Ness Botanical Gardens Vis. Cen.
3E 45
NESSHOLT **2D 44**
NESTON **5C 38**
Neston Grn. CH66: Gt Sut 3D **48**
(not continuous)
Neston Recreation Cen. 4D 38
Neston Rd. CH63: Thorn H 6H **33**
CH64: Ness 2D **44**
CH64: Nest 6H **33**
CH64: Will 5A **40**
Neston Station (Rail) **5C 38**
Neston St. L4: Walt 2H **7**
Netherby St. L8: Liv 4H **23**
Netherfield Cl. CH43: Noct 3A **20**
Netherfield Rd. Nth. L5: Liv 5G **7**
Netherfield Rd. Sth.
L5: Liv 1G **15**
Netherpool Rd. CH66: Ell P 6F **43**
Netherton Rd. CH46: More 5E **11**
Netley St. L4: Kirk 3G **7**
Neva Av. CH46: More 5D **10**
Neville Cl. CH43: Noct 3A **20**
Neville Rd. CH44: Wall 1E **13**
CH62: Brom 4C **36**
Nevin St. L6: Liv 2H **15**
New Acres Cl. CH43: Bid 5A **12**
Newark Cl. CH43: Noct 3A **20**
Newark St. L4: Walt 2G **7**
New Bird St. L1: Liv 6F **15**
Newbold Cres.
CH48: W Kir 4G **17**
Newbridge Cl.
CH49: W'chu 4H **19**
Newbridge Rd. CH65: Ell P 3D **50**
NEW BRIGHTON 2F 5
New Brighton Station (Rail) **3E 5**
Newburn CH43: O'ton 2F **21**
Newburns La. CH43: O'ton 4F **21**
Newburn St. L4: Walt 1H **7**
Newbury Way CH46: Leas 2F **11**
Newby St. L4: Walt 3H **7**
New Chester Rd.
CH41: Birk, Tran 2B **22**
CH42: R Ferr 4B **22**
CH62: Brom, East, Port S
4A **30**
CH62: New F 4B **22**
CH66: Hoot 3A **42**
Newdales Cl. CH43: Bid 5A **12**
Newell Rd. CH44: Wall 6F **5**
New Extension Quay
CH65: Ell P 1G **43**
NEW FERRY **2H** 29
New Ferry By-Pass
CH62: New F, Port S 1H **29**
New Ferry Rd.
CH62: New F 2H **29**
New Grosvenor Rd.
CH65: Ell P 6H **43**
New Hall La. CH47: Hoy 1D **16**
New Hall Manor
CH64: Nest 5G **33**
New Hall Pl. L3: Liv 3D **14**
Newhall St. L1: Liv 6F **15**
Newhaven Rd. CH45: New B 4G **5**
New Hedley Gro. L5: Liv 6E **7**
New Henderson St. L8: Liv 1G **23**
New Heyes CH64: Nest 4C **38**
New Hey La. CH64: Will 6B **40**
New Hey Rd. CH49: W'chu 3H **19**
Newhope Rd. CH41: Birk 6G **13**
New Houses La.
CH64: Lit N 3C **44**
Newington L1: Liv 4F **15**

Oxford Ho.—Pool La.

Oxford Ho. *L20: Boot* *1G 7*
(off Fernhill Rd.)
Oxford Rd. CH44: Wall 1G 13
Oxford St. L7: Liv 4H 15
(not continuous)
Oxford St. E. L7: Liv 4H 15
Oxley Av. CH46: Leas 2H 11
OXTON 3D 20
Oxton Grn. CH66: Gt Sut 3D 48
Oxton Rd. CH41: Birk 2G 21
CH43: O'ton 2G 21
CH44: Wall 2F 13
Oxton St. L4: Walt 3H 7

P

Pacific Rd. CH41: Birk 6B 14
Padbury St. L8: Liv 2H 23
Paddington L7: Liv 4H 15
(not continuous)
Paddock, The CH46: More 6C 10
CH49: Upton 2H 19
CH60: Hes 3E 33
CH66: Gt Sut 4D 48
Paddock Dr. CH64: Park 3B 38
Padstow Rd. CH49: Grea 4C 18
Page Wlk. L3: Liv 2G 15
(not continuous)
Pagewood Cl. CH43: Noct 3B 20
Paignton Rd. CH45: Wall 5D 4
Painswick Rd.
CH66: Gt Sut 5E 49
Paisley Av. CH62: East 1G 41
Paisley St. L3: Liv 2D 14
Palace Hey CH64: Ness 2E 45
Palatine Rd. CH44: Wall 3H 13
CH62: Brom 2A 36
Palermo Cl. CH44: Wall 3H 13
Paley Cl. L4: Walt 4H 7
Pall Mall L3: Liv 2D 14
Pall Mall Cen. L3: Liv 2D 14
Palm Ct. *L8: Liv* *3H 23*
(off Weller Way)
Palmer Cl. CH43: Noct 4B 20
Palmerston Rd. CH44: Wall 1D 12
Palmerston St.
CH42: R Ferr 5B 22
Palm Gro. CH43: O'ton 1E 21
CH66: Whit 6G 49
Palm Hill CH43: O'ton 3F 21
Palmwood Cl. CH43: Pren 6C 20
Paltridge Way CH61: Pens 5B 26
Pansy St. L5: Kirk 4F 7
Parade, The CH64: Park 4A 38
Paradise St. L1: Liv 5E 15
Park Av. CH44: Wall 2H 13
Parkbridge Rd. CH42: Tran 4G 21
Parkbury Ct. CH43: O'ton 4E 21
Park Cl. CH41: Birk 1G 21
Park Ct. CH48: W Kir 5C 16
Parkdale CH48: Caldy 3B 24
Park Dr. CH41: Birk 6F 13
CH43: C'ton 6E 13
CH65: Whit 4H 49
Parkend Rd. CH42: Tran 4G 21
Parker St. L1: Liv 4F 15
Parkfield Av. CH41: Birk 1H 21
Parkfield Dr. CH44: Wall 1F 13
CH65: Whit 5G 49
Parkfield Pl. CH41: Birk 1H 21
Parkfield Rd. CH63: Beb 6G 29
PARKGATE 4A 38
Parkgate Ho. CH64: Park 3A 38
(off Greenway)
Parkgate La. CH64: Nest 6G 33
Parkgate Rd. CH1: W'bnk 4D 46
CH64: Nest 5B 38
CH66: Led 4D 46
Park Gro. CH41: Birk 2H 21
Park Hill Ct. L8: Liv 3H 23
Park Hill Rd. L8: Liv 3H 23
Parkhill Rd. CH42: Tran 4G 21
Parkhurst Rd. CH42: Tran 5G 21
Parkland Cl. L8: Liv 2H 23
Parkland Ct. CH43: Bid 5A 12
Parklands CH66: Lit Sut 2C 48
Parklands Ct. *CH49: W'chu* *5G 19*
(off Childwall Grn.)
Parklands Dr. CH60: Hes 5D 32
Parklands Gdns.
CH66: Lit Sut 1D 48
Parklands Vw.
CH66: Lit Sut 1D 48
Park La. CH47: Meols 4A 10
L1: Liv 5E 15
Parklea CH66: Lit Sut 1D 48
Park Pl. L8: Liv 1G 23
Park Rd. CH42: Tran 4A 22
CH44: Wall 2G 13
CH47: Meols 4G 9
CH48: W Kir 5C 16
CH60: Hes 2D 32
CH62: East 5D 36
CH62: Port S 4H 29
CH64: Will 5D 40
CH65: Ell P 3A 50
(not continuous)
L8: Liv 2H 23
Park Rd. E. CH41: Birk 1G 21
Park Rd. Nth. CH41: Birk 6D 12
Park Rd. Sth. CH43: C'ton 1F 21
Park Road Sports Cen. 2H 23
Park Rd. W. CH43: C'ton 6D 12
Parkside CH44: Wall 2G 13
Parkside Cl. CH63: Beb 3G 29
CH64: Park 5B 38
Parkside Rd. CH42: Tran 4A 22
CH63: Beb 3G 29
Parkside St. L6: Liv 2H 15
Parkstone Rd. CH42: Tran 4G 21
Park St. CH41: Birk 1H 21
(not continuous)
CH44: Wall 1G 13
CH64: Nest 5C 38
L8: Liv 2F 23
Park Va. CH64: Nest 6D 38
Parkvale Av. CH43: Pren 1G 27
Park Vw. CH62: Brom 3A 36
Parkview Cl. CH41: Birk 6G 13
Parkview Ct. CH60: Hes 3B 32
Park Way L8: Liv 6H 15
(not continuous)
Parkway CH45: Wall 4C 4
CH47: Meols 5G 9
CH61: Irby 2B 26
Parkway Cl. CH61: Irby 2B 26
Park W. CH60: Hes 4H 31
Parkwood Cl. CH62: Brom 2B 36
Parliament Cl. L1: Liv 6G 15
Parliament Pl. L8: Liv 6H 15
Parliament St. L8: Liv 6F 15
Parliament Way
CH66: Gt Sut 6A 48
Parnell Rd. CH63: Spit 6G 29
Parr Gro. CH49: Grea 3C 18
Parr's Rd. CH43: O'ton 4F 21
Parr St. L1: Liv 5F 15
Parry St. CH44: Wall 3H 13
Pasture Av. CH46: More 3E 11
Pasture Cres. CH46: More 4E 11
Pasture Rd. CH46: More 2D 10
Pastures, The CH48: W Kir 5H 17
Paterson St. CH41: Birk 1G 21
Patmos Cl. L5: Liv 5G 7
Paton Cl. CH48: W Kir 4F 17
Patricia Av. CH41: Birk 4D 12
Patten St. CH41: Birk 5E 13
Patterdale Rd. CH63: Beb 6F 29
Paul Orr Ct. L3: Liv 1E 15
Paulsfield Dr. CH46: More 6E 11
Paul St. L3: Liv 2E 15
Paulton Cl. L8: Liv 3H 23
Peach St. L7: Liv 4H 15
Pearson Rd. CH42: Tran 3A 22
Pear Tree Cl. CH60: Hes 2E 33
Peartree Way
CH66: Gt Sut 6E 49
Peckforton Dr.
CH66: Gt Sut 4E 49
Pecksniff Cl. L8: Liv 2H 23
Peebles Cl. CH66: Lit Sut 1H 47
Peel Av. CH42: Tran 4B 22
Peel Pl. L8: Liv 6H 15
Peel St. L8: Liv 3H 23
Peers Wood Ct.
CH64: Lit N 2C 44
Pelham Rd. CH44: Wall 2E 13
Pemberton Cl. CH64: Will 5C 40
Pemberton Rd.
CH49: W'chu 4H 19
Pembridge Ct. CH65: Ell P 4C 50
Pembridge Gdns.
CH65: Ell P 4C 50
Pembroke Av. CH46: More 6E 11
Pembroke Ct. CH41: Tran 3A 22
Pembroke Dr. CH65: Whit 4G 49
Pembroke Gdns.
L3: Liv 3H 15
Pembroke Pl. L3: Liv 3G 15
Pembroke Rd. L20: Boot 1E 7
Pembroke St. L3: Liv 3H 15
Pendennis Rd. CH44: Wall 2G 13
Pendle Cl. CH49: Upton 1E 19
CH66: Lit Sut 1H 47
Pengwern St. L8: Liv 2H 23
Pengwern Ter. CH45: New B 4G 5
Peninsula Cl. CH45: Wall 3C 4
Penistone Dr.
CH66: Lit Sut 2B 48
Penkett Ct. CH45: Wall 5G 5
Penkett Gdns. CH45: Wall 5G 5
Penkett Gro. CH45: Wall 5G 5
Penkett Rd. CH45: Wall 5F 5
Penmon Dr. CH61: Pens 6B 26
Penn Gdns. CH65: Ell P 2H 49
Pennine Rd. CH42: Tran 6G 21
CH44: Wall 1D 12
Pennine Wlk. CH66: Lit Sut 2B 48
Pennington Grn.
CH66: Gt Sut 4C 48
Pennington St. L4: Walt 1H 7
Pennystone Cl.
CH49: Upton 1D 18
Penrhos Rd. CH47: Hoy 1C 16
Penrhyd Rd. CH61: Irby 4H 25
Penrhyn Av. CH61: Thing 3C 26
Penrhyn St. L5: Liv 6F 7
Penrith St. CH41: Birk 2G 21
Penrose St. L5: Liv 5G 7
Pensall Dr. CH61: Hes 1B 32
PENSBY 5C 26
Pensby Cl. CH61: Thing 4C 26
Pensby Dr. CH66: Gt Sut 3D 48
Pensby Hall La. CH61: Hes 1B 32
Pensby Rd. CH60: Hes 3B 32
CH61: Pens, Thing 4C 26
Pensby St. CH41: Birk 5F 13
Pentland Av. L4: Walt 2H 7
Penuel Rd. L4: Walt 1H 7
Peover St. L3: Liv 2F 15
Percival Rd. CH65: Ell P 1H 49
Percy Rd. CH44: Wall 3H 13
Percy St. L8: Liv 6H 15
Perrin Rd. CH45: Wall 6C 4
Perry St. L8: Liv 1F 23
Pershore Ho. CH42: Tran 6F 21
Peterborough Cl.
CH66: Gt Sut 6A 48
Peter Price's La.
CH63: High B 5E 29
Peter Rd. L4: Walt 1G 7
(not continuous)
Peter's La. L1: Liv 4F 15
Peter St. CH44: Wall 3A 14
L1: Liv 3F 15
Peterswood Ct. CH64: Lit N 2C 44
Peterwood CH42: R Ferr 6C 22
Petton St. L5: Liv 5H 7
Peveril St. L9: Walt 1H 7
Philharmonic Ct. *L7: Liv* *5H 15*
(off Caledonia St.)
Philharmonic Hall 5H 15
Philip Leverhume Lodge
CH62: Port S 3H 29
Philips La. CH66: Gt Sut 3C 48
Phillips St. L3: Liv 2E 15
Phillips Way CH60: Hes 3A 32
Phythian St. L6: Liv 2H 15
Pickerill Rd. CH49: Grea 4D 18
Pickering Rd. CH45: New B 3F 5
Pickmere Dr. CH62: East 2H 41
(not continuous)
Pickop St. L3: Liv 2E 15
Pickwick St. L8: Liv 1H 23
Picton Cl. CH43: O'ton 3D 20
CH62: East 2F 41
Picton Hall *3F 15*
(off Cuerden St.)
Pikes Hey Rd. CH48: Caldy 2D 24
Pilgrim St. CH41: Birk 1B 22
L1: Liv 5G 15
Pimhill Cl. L8: Liv 1H 23
Pincroft Way L4: Kirk 4F 7
Pine Av. CH63: Beb 6F 29
Pine Ct. CH41: Birk 1H 21
L8: Liv *3H 23*
(off Byles St.)
Pinedale Cl. CH43: Noct 3B 20
CH66: Whit 6A 48
Pine Gro. CH66: Whit 6G 49
Pinehey CH64: Nest 4B 38
Pine M. L1: Liv 6G 15
Pineridge Cl. CH62: Spit 1A 36
Pine Rd. CH60: Hes 2E 33
Pines, The CH63: Spit 6H 29
Pine Tree Av. CH43: Noct 3A 20
Pine Tree Cl. CH46: More 5F 11
Pinetree Ct. CH44: Wall 6D 4
Pinetree Dr. CH48: W Kir 6F 17
Pinetree Gro. CH46: More 5F 11
Pine Vw. Dr. CH61: Hes 1C 32
Pine Wlk. Ridge
CH42: Tran 1C 28
Pine Walks CH42: Tran 6F 21
CH48: W Kir 6F 17
Pine Way CH60: Hes 1A 32
Pinewood Dr. CH60: Hes 3D 32
Pinfold Ct. CH48: W Kir 3C 16
Pinfold La. CH48: W Kir 3C 16
Pipers, The CH60: Hes 2H 31
Piper's Cl. CH60: Hes 3H 31
Piper's End CH60: Hes 3H 31
Pipers La. CH60: Hes 1G 31
(not continuous)
CH64: Pudd 6C 46
Pipistrelle Ri. CH43: Noct 3C 20
Pitch Cl. CH49: Grea 3D 18
Pitt St. L1: Liv 5F 15
Plane Tree Rd.
CH63: High B 5E 29
Plantation Bus. Pk.
CH62: Brom 1D 36
Plantation Dr. CH66: Ell P 6E 43
Plantation Rd. CH62: Brom 2D 36
Planters, The CH49: Grea 3C 18
Platt Gro. CH42: R Ferr 1G 29
Pleasant Hill St. L8: Liv 1F 23
Pleasant St. CH45: New B 4F 5
L3: Liv 4G 15
L20: Boot 1D 6
Pleasant Vw. L20: Boot 1D 6
Pleasington Cl. CH43: Noct 3C 20
Pleasington Dr.
CH43: Noct 3C 20
Pleck Rd. CH65: Whit 5G 49
Plemston Ct. CH66: Ell P 5F 43
Ploughmans Cl.
CH66: Gt Sut 6A 48
Ploughmans Way
CH66: Gt Sut 6A 48
Plumer St. CH41: Birk 5E 13
Plumpton St. L6: Liv 1H 15
Plymyard Av. CH62: Brom 5A 36
Plymyard Cl. CH62: Brom 6B 36
Plymyard Copse
CH62: Brom 6B 36
Poets Cnr. CH62: Port S 4H 29
Polden Cl. CH66: Lit Sut 1A 48
POLL HILL 1B 32
Poll Hill Rd. CH60: Hes 2B 32
Pollitt Sq. CH62: New F 1A 30
Pomfret St. L8: Liv 1H 23
Pomona St. L3: Liv 4G 15
Pond Vw. Cl. CH60: Hes 3E 33
Ponsonby Rd. CH45: Wall 6C 4
Pool Bank CH62: Port S 2H 29
Poolbank Rd. CH62: New F 2H 29
Poole Hall Ind. Est.
CH66: Ell P 5F 43
(not continuous)
Poole Hall La. CH66: Ell P 5E 43
Poole Hall Rd. CH65: Ell P 5F 43
Poole Rd. CH44: Wall 6H 5
Pool La. CH49: W'chu 5G 19
CH62: Brom 4A 30

Redbrook Cl.—Royal Quay

Redbrook Cl. CH62: Brom 5B **36**
Redburn Cl. L8: Liv 3H **23**
Redcap Cl. CH45: Wall 3C **4**
Redcar Dr. CH62: East 6B **36**
Redcar Rd. CH45: Wall 5B **4**
Redcote Ct. CH48: W Kir 6C **16**
Redcroft CH49: Grea 4C **18**
Red Cross St. L1: Liv 4E **15**
Redditch Cl. CH49: Grea 3C **18**
Redfern St. L20: Kirk 3E **7**
Redfield Cl. CH44: Wall 1H **13**
Redford Cl. CH49: Grea 3C **18**
Red Hill Rd. CH63: Store . . . 4B **28**
Redhills M. CH65: Ell P 1H **49**
Redhouse Bank
CH48: W Kir 4C **16**
Redhouse La. CH48: W Kir . . 4C **16**
Red Lion La. CH66: Lit Sut . . 6C **42**
Redmere Dr. CH60: Hes 3F **33**
Redmont St. CH41: Tran 3A **22**
Red Pike CH66: Lit Sut 6D **42**
Redstone Cl. CH47: Meols . . . 5F **9**
Redstone Dr. CH60: Hes 2G **31**
Redstone Pk. CH45: Wall 3D **4**
Redstone Ri. CH43: Noct . . . 1B **20**
Redvers Av. CH66: Hoot 3A **42**
Redwood Cl. CH43: O'ton . . . 5D **20**
Redwood Ct. *L8: Liv* *3H 23*
(off Byles St.)
Redwood Dr. CH66: Gt Sut . . 6F **49**
Reeds Av. E. CH46: Leas 2F **11**
Reeds Av. W. CH46: Leas . . . 2F **11**
Reeds La.
CH46: Leas, More 1F **11**
Reedville CH43: O'ton 2F **21**
Reedville Gro. CH46: Leas . . . 3F **11**
Reedville Rd. CH63: Beb 4F **29**
Regal Cl. CH66: Gt Sut 4E **49**
Regal Wlk. L4: Walt 4G **7**
Regent Rd. CH45: Wall 5B **4**
L3: Liv 1D **6**
L5: Liv, Kirk 1D **6**
Regents Cl. CH61: Thing 4D **26**
Regent St. CH65: Ell P 2F **49**
L3: Liv 1D **14**
Regents Way CH63: High B . . 1D **28**
Reid Ct. CH66: Lit Sut 6C **42**
Reins Cft. CH64: Nest 4C **38**
Rendal Cl. L5: Liv 6H **7**
Rendelsham Cl.
CH49: Upton 2E **19**
Rendel St. CH41: Birk 6H **13**
Renfrew Av. CH62: East 6C **36**
Renfrew St. L7: Liv 3H **15**
Renshaw St. L1: Liv 4G **15**
Repton Rd. CH65: Ell P 3B **50**
Reservoir Rd. CH42: Tran . . . 6F **21**
Reservoir Rd. Nth.
CH42: Tran 6F **21**
Reservoir St. L6: Liv 1H **15**
Rest Hill Rd. CH63: Store . . . 4B **28**
Rhodesway CH60: Hes 4D **32**
Rhona Cl. CH63: East 1E **41**
Rhuddlan Ct. CH65: Ell P 5B **50**
Rhum Cl. CH65: Ell P 6A **50**
Rhyl St. L8: Liv 2G **23**
Rialto Cl. L8: Liv 6H **15**
Ribblesdale CH65: Whit 4H **49**
Ribblesdale Cl. CH62: East . . . 6D **36**
Ribble St. CH41: Birk 4D **12**
Rice Hey Rd. CH44: Wall 6G **5**
Rice La. CH44: Wall 6G **5**
(not continuous)
L9: Walt 1H **7**
Rice St. L1: Liv 5G **15**
Richard Allen Way L5: Liv . . . 1G **15**
Richard Chubb Dr.
CH44: Wall 5H **5**
Richardson Rd.
CH42: R Ferr 6A **22**
Richmond Cl. CH63: Beb 3F **29**
Richmond Ct. CH65: Ell P . . . 4B **50**
Richmond Ho. L3: Liv 3D **14**
Richmond Pde. *L3: Liv* *3D 14*
(off Rumford Pl.)
Richmond Rd. CH63: Beb . . . 3F **29**
Richmond Row L3: Liv 2G **15**
Richmond St. CH45: New B . . . 2F **5**
L1: Liv 4F **15**
Richmond Way CH61: Hes . . . 1B **32**
CH61: Thing 3C **26**
Rich Vw. CH43: O'ton 4F **21**
Rickaby Cl. CH63: Brom 3A **36**
Rickman St. L4: Kirk 3F **7**
Riddings, The CH65: Whit . . . 3H **49**
Ridge, The CH60: Hes 1H **31**
Ridgefield Rd. CH61: Pens . . 4B **26**
Ridgemere Rd.
CH61: Pens 4B **26**
Ridgeview Rd. CH43: Noct . . 2B **20**
Ridgeway, The CH47: Meols . . 6G **9**
CH60: Hes 4D **32**
CH63: High B 1D **28**
Ridgeway Cl. CH66: Gt Sut . . 5C **48**
Ridgewood Dr. CH61: Pens . . 5B **26**
Ridings, The CH43: Noct 2B **20**
Ridings Hey CH43: Noct 3B **20**
Riding St. L3: Liv 3G **15**
Ridley Gro. CH48: W Kir 4C **16**
Ridley St. CH43: O'ton 2G **21**
Rigby Dr. CH49: Grea 5D **18**
Rigby St. L3: Liv 3D **14**
Rimmer St. L3: Liv 3G **15**
Ring Rd. CH1: Back 6A **48**
Ringway CH64: Nest 4C **38**
CH66: Gt Sut 3E **49**
Ringways CH62: Brom 6B **30**
Ringwood CH43: O'ton 4E **21**
Ripon Av. CH66: Lit Sut 2C **48**
Ripon Rd. CH45: Wall 5C **4**
Ripon St. CH41: Tran 3A **22**
L4: Walt 2H **7**
Rishton Cl. L5: Liv 6H **7**
Rishton St. L5: Liv 6H **7**
Rivacre Brow CH66: Ell P 6E **43**
Rivacre Bus. Cen.
CH66: Ell P 2E **49**
Rivacre Rd. CH62: East 6E **37**
CH66: Ell P 6E **43**
Rivacre Valley Country Pk.
. . . . 5E 43
Riva La. CH60: Hes 1A **32**
Riveacre Rd. CH65: Hoot . . . 3C **42**
Riverbank Cl. CH60: Hes 5B **32**
Riverbank Rd. CH60: Hes 5B **32**
CH62: Brom 6C **30**
River Gro. CH62: New F 1H **29**
Riverpark Gdns. *L8: Liv* *1G 23*
(off Hyslop St.)
Riversdale Rd. CH44: Wall . . . 1H **13**
CH48: W Kir 5C **16**
Riverside CH48: W Kir 6D **16**
CH62: Port S 4H **29**
Riverside Bowl 2F 5
Riverside Ct. CH62: New F . . . 1H **29**
Riverside Dr. L3: Liv 4G **23**
L17: Aig 4G **23**
Riverside Ho. CH41: Birk 4B **14**
Riverside Wlk. CH64: Lit N . . . 2B **44**
L3: Liv 5D **14**
River Vw. CH62: New F 1A **30**
Riverview Gdns.
CH42: R Ferr 5B **22**
Riverview Rd. CH44: Wall 2A **14**
CH62: Brom 1E **37**
CH64: Lit N 2D **44**
Riverview Wlk. L8: Liv 3H **23**
Riverwood Rd.
CH62: Brom 2D **36**
Riviera Dr. CH42: R Ferr 6H **21**
Rivington Av. CH43: Noct 3C **20**
Rivington Rd. CH44: Wall 2G **13**
CH65: Ell P 2H **49**
Robert Dr. CH49: Grea 4E **19**
Robertson St. L8: Liv 2G **23**
Roberts St. L3: Liv 2D **14**
Robert St. CH41: Birk 6H **13**
Robins Cft. CH66: Gt Sut 5F **49**
Robinson M. *CH41: Birk* *1B 22*
(off Gertrude St.)
Robin Way CH49: W'chu 5H **19**
Robsart St. L5: Liv 6G **7**
Robson St. L5: Liv 4H **7**
Rocastle Cl. L6: Liv 2H **15**
Rochester Dr. CH65: Ell P . . . 5B **50**
Rochester Rd.
CH42: R Ferr 5B **22**
Rock Av. CH60: Hes 2B **32**
Rock Bank CH49: Upton 2G **19**
Rock Cl. CH42: R Ferr 5B **22**
Rock Farm Cl. CH64: Lit N . . . 1E **45**
Rock Farm Dr. CH64: Lit N . . . 1E **45**
Rock Farm Gro.
CH64: Lit N 1E **45**
ROCK FERRY **5B 22**
Rock Ferry By-Pass
CH42: R Ferr 4C **22**
Rock Ferry Station (Rail) 5B 22
Rockfield Rd. L4: Walt 4H **7**
Rockland Rd. CH45: Wall 4D **4**
Rocklands Av. CH63: Beb 2G **29**
Rocklands La.
CH63: Thorn H 4C **34**
Rock La. E. CH42: R Ferr 6C **22**
(not continuous)
Rock La. W. CH42: R Ferr 6B **22**
Rocklee Gdns. CH64: Lit N . . . 1E **45**
Rockley St. L4: Kirk 3G **7**
(not continuous)
Rock Pk. CH42: R Ferr 5C **22**
(not continuous)
Rock Pk. Rd. CH42: R Ferr . . . 6D **22**
Rockpoint Av. CH45: New B . . . 4G **5**
Rock Retail Pk. CH41: Birk . . . 2A **22**
Rock Vw. L5: Liv 5G **7**
Rockville St. CH42: R Ferr . . . 5B **22**
Rockybank Rd. CH42: Tran . . . 4H **21**
Rocky La. CH60: Hes 3B **32**
Rocky La. Sth. CH60: Hes 3C **32**
Roderick Rd. L4: Walt 1H **7**
Roderick St. L3: Liv 2G **15**
Rodney St. CH41: Birk 2H **21**
L1: Liv 5G **15**
Roe All. L1: Liv 4F **15**
Roe St. *L1: Liv* *3F 15*
(off Queen Sq.)
Roften Works Ind. Est.
CH66: Hoot 5F **41**
Rokeby Cl. L3: Liv 1G **15**
Rokeby St. L3: Liv 2G **15**
Roker Av. CH44: Wall 2E **13**
Roklis Ct. CH49: Upton 3G **19**
Roland Av. CH63: High B 3D **28**
Rolleston Dr. CH45: Wall 4D **4**
CH63: Beb 5G **29**
Rollo St. L4: Kirk 4F **7**
Roman Ct. CH64: Lit N 6D **38**
Roman Rd. CH43: Pren 1A **28**
CH47: Meols 4F **9**
CH63: Store 2A **28**
Romiley Rd. CH66: Ell P 1E **49**
Romley St. L4: Walt 1H **7**
Romney Cl. CH64: Lit N 6C **38**
Romney Cft. CH64: Lit N 6D **38**
Romney Way CH64: Lit N 6D **38**
Rona Av. CH65: Ell P 6A **50**
Ronaldsway CH49: Upton 1F **19**
CH60: Hes 5B **32**
Rone Cl. CH46: More 5D **10**
Rooks Way CH60: Hes 3A **32**
Roper St. L8: Liv 2H **23**
Ropewalk, The CH64: Park . . . 4A **38**
Ropewalks Sq. *L1: Liv* *5G 15*
(off Bold St.)
Rosalind Av. CH63: High B . . . 2E **29**
Rosalind Way L20: Kirk 2F **7**
Rosclare Dr. CH45: Wall 5D **4**
Roscoe La. L1: Liv 5G **15**
Roscoe Pl. L1: Liv 4G **15**
Roscoe St. L1: Liv 5G **15**
Roscommon St. L5: Liv 1G **15**
(not continuous)
Roscote, The CH60: Hes 4B **32**
Roscote Cl. CH60: Hes 4B **32**
Roseacre CH48: W Kir 4C **16**
Roseate Ct. CH45: Wall 3C **4**
Rosebery Av. CH44: Wall 1G **13**
Rosebery Gro. CH42: Tran 5F **21**
Rosebery St. L8: Liv 6H **15**
Rosebrae Ct. CH41: Birk 6B **14**
CH60: Hes 2C **32**
Rose Ct. CH41: Birk 1H **21**
Rosecroft CH62: Brom 5A **36**
Rosecroft Ct. CH47: Hoy 1C **16**
Rosedale Rd. CH42: Tran 4A **22**
Rosefield Av. CH63: High B . . . 2E **29**
Rose Gdns. CH64: Lit N 1D **44**
Rose Hill L3: Liv 2F **15**
Roselands Ct.
CH42: R Ferr 6A **22**
Roselee Ct. CH42: R Ferr 6C **22**
Rosemary Cl. CH43: Bid 5C **12**
Rosemead Av. CH61: Pens . . . 5B **26**
Rosemere Dr. CH1: Back 6A **48**
Rose Mt. CH43: O'ton 4F **21**
Rosemount Cl.
CH43: O'ton 4E **21**
Rose Mt. Dr. CH45: Wall 5E **5**
Rose Pl. CH42: Tran 3H **21**
L3: Liv 2F **15**
(not continuous)
Rose St. *L1: Liv* *3F 15*
(off St George's Pl.)
Rose Va. L5: Liv 6G **7**
(Gt. Homer St., not continuous)
L5: Liv 6G **7**
(Netherfield Rd. N.)
Rosewood Dr. CH46: More . . . 5B **10**
Roslin Rd. CH43: O'ton 3F **21**
CH61: Irby 3H **25**
Roslyn St. CH42: Tran 4B **22**
Rossall Ct. CH46: Leas 3F **11**
Rossall Gro. CH66: Lit Sut . . . 1D **48**
Rossall Rd. CH46: More 4F **11**
Ross Av. CH46: Leas 1A **12**
Rossbank Rd. CH65: Ell P 6G **43**
Rosscliffe Rd. CH65: Ell P 6G **43**
Ross Dr. CH66: Gt Sut 2C **48**
Rossendale Cl. CH43: Noct . . . 3B **20**
Rossfield Rd. CH65: Ell P 6G **43**
Rosslyn Cres. CH46: More . . . 5E **11**
Rosslyn Dr. CH46: More 5E **11**
Rosslyn Pk. CH46: More 6E **11**
Rossmore Bus. Pk.
CH65: Ell P 6H **43**
Rossmore Gdns.
CH66: Lit Sut 1D **48**
Rossmore Ind. Est.
CH65: Ell P 6G **43**
Rossmore Rd. E.
CH65: Ell P 6F **43**
Rossmore Rd. W.
CH66: Ell P, Lit Sut 6D **42**
Rossmore Trad. Est.
CH65: Ell P 1G **49**
Rossmount Rd. CH65: Ell P . . . 1G **49**
Ross Rd. CH65: Ell P 1G **49**
Ross Tower Ct.
CH45: New B 3G **5**
Rosswood Rd. CH65: Ell P . . . 1G **49**
Rostherne Av. CH44: Wall 2E **13**
CH66: Gt Sut 3E **49**
Rothbury Cl. CH46: More 5C **10**
Rother Dr. CH65: Ell P 6G **43**
Rother Dr. Bus. Pk.
CH65: Ell P 6G **43**
Rotherwood CH43: Noct 2B **20**
Rotherwood Cl.
CH63: High B 3D **28**
Rothesay Ct. CH63: Beb 5F **29**
Rothesay Dr. CH62: East 1G **41**
Rothesay Gdns.
CH43: Pren 6D **20**
Rothsay Cl. L5: Liv 1G **15**
Rotunda St. L5: Liv 6F **7**
Rowan Ct. CH49: Grea 5B **18**
CH63: High B 3D **28**
Rowan Gro. CH63: High B 5E **29**
Rowan Tree Cl. CH49: Grea . . . 4C **18**
Rowson St. CH45: New B 2F **5**
Rowton Cl. CH43: O'ton 4D **20**
Roxburgh Av. CH42: Tran 5H **21**
Roxburgh Rd.
CH66: Lit Sut 1H **47**
Roxburgh St. L4: Kirk 1G **7**
L20: Boot 1G **7**
Royal, The CH47: Hoy 1B **16**
Royal Court Theatre 3F 15
ROYAL LIVERPOOL DENTAL
HOSPITAL 3H 15
Royal Liverpool Golf Course
. . . . 2B 16
ROYAL LIVERPOOL UNIVERISTY
HOSPITAL 3H 15
Royal Mail St. L3: Liv 4G **15**
Royal Quay L3: Liv 5E **15**

Royal Shop. Arc.
CH64: Nest 6C 38
Royal Standard Way
CH42: Tran 4B 22
Royal St. L4: Walt 4G 7
Royden Av. CH44: Wall 6H 5
Royden Rd. CH49: Upton 1E 19
Royden Way L3: Liv 4G 23
Royston Av. CH44: Wall 1H 13
Royston Cl. CH66: Gt Sut 4F 49
Rubbing Stone
CH48: Caldy 3B 24
(not continuous)
Ruby St. L8: Liv 4H 23
Rudd St. CH47: Hoy 6D 8
Rudgrave M. CH44: Wall 6H 5
Rudgrave Pl. CH44: Wall 6H 5
Rudgrave Sq. CH44: Wall 6H 5
Rudstone Cl. CH66: Lit Sut . . .2B 48
Rufford Rd. CH44: Wall 2F 13
Rugby Rd. CH44: Wall 6D 4
CH65: Ell P 4A 50
Rugby Wlk. CH65: Ell P 4B 50
Rullerton Rd. CH44: Wall 1E 13
Rumford Pl. L3: Liv 3D 14
Rumford St. L2: Liv 3E 15
Rumney Pl. L4: Kirk 3F 7
(not continuous)
Rumney Rd. L4: Kirk 3G 7
Rumney Rd. W. L4: Kirk 3F 7
Rundle St. CH41: Birk 5E 13
Runnell, The CH64: Nest 2B 38
Rupert Dr. L6: Liv 2H 15
Rushgreen Cl. CH43: Bid 6A 12
Ruskin Av. CH42: R Ferr 6B 22
CH44: Wall 2E 13
Ruskin Cl. L20: Boot 1E 7
Ruskin Dr. CH65: Ell P 4B 50
Ruskin St. L4: Kirk 2G 7
Ruskin Way CH41: Birk 4B 20
Rusland Av. CH61: Pens 5B 26
Russell Pl. L3: Liv 4G 15
Russell Rd. CH42: R Ferr 4B 22
(not continuous)
CH44: Wall 6C 4
Russell St. CH41: Birk 6A 14
L3: Liv 3G 15
Ruthin Cl. CH65: Ell P 4B 50
Rutland Cl. L5: Liv 6H 7
Rutter St. L8: Liv 2G 23
Rycroft Rd. CH44: Wall 2G 13
CH47: Meols 5G 9
Rydal Av. CH43: Noct 2A 20
Rydal Bank CH44: Wall 1G 13
CH63: Beb 2G 29
Rydal Cl. CH61: Pens 5C 26
CH64: Lit N 1D 44
CH65: Ell P 5A 50
Ryecroft Rd. CH60: Hes 4E 33
Ryland Pk. CH61: Thing 4C 26
Rylands Hey CH49: Grea 3D 18
Ryleys Gdns. L2: Liv 3E 15
Rymer Gro. L4: Walt 2H 7

S

Saddlestone Gro. L8: Liv . . .2G 23
St Agnes Rd. L4: Kirk 3F 7
St Aidan's Ct. CH43: C'ton . . .1D 20
St Aidans Ter. CH43: C'ton . . .1D 20
L5: Kirk 5F 7
(off Latham St.)
St Albans Ct. L5: Liv 6E 7
St Albans Rd. CH43: C'ton . . .6E 13
CH44: Wall 1F 13
L20: Boot 1E 7
St Alban's Sq. L20: Boot 1E 7
St Alexander Cl. L20: Kirk . . .2F 7
St Ambrose Way
L5: Liv 1G 15
St Andrews Ct. CH43: Noct . .1B 20
CH65: Ell P 5C 50
St Andrews Gdns. L3: Liv . . .3G 15
St Andrews Rd.
CH43: O'ton 1F 21
CH63: Beb 5G 29
CH65: Ell P 4B 50
St Andrew St. L3: Liv 4G 15

St Annes Cl. CH43: Birk 6H 13
St Annes Ct. L3: Liv 2G 15
(off St Anne Rd.)
St Annes Gro. CH43: Birk . . .5G 13
St Anne's Ho. L20: Boot 1E 7
St Annes Pl. CH41: Birk 5G 13
St Annes Ter. CH43: Birk 6G 13
St Anne St. CH41: Birk 5G 13
(not continuous)
L3: Liv 2F 15
St Annes Way CH41: Birk . . .6H 13
St Anthony's La.
L5: Liv 6F 7
St Asaph Rd. CH66: Gt Sut . .6A 48
St Augustine St.
L5: Liv 6F 7
St Austell Cl. CH46: More . . .4B 10
St Austells Rd. L4: Walt 1G 7
St Bartholomew Rd.
L3: Liv 2E 15
St Bride's Rd. CH44: Wall 6H 5
St Bride St. L8: Liv 5H 15
St Bridget's La.
CH48: W Kir 6D 16
St Brigids Cres. L5: Liv 6E 7
St Catherines Gdns.
CH42: Tran 3H 21
ST CATHERINE'S HOSPITAL
(BIRKENHEAD) 3H 21
St Catherine's Rd. L20: Boot . .1E 7
St Columbas Cl. CH44: Wall . .6H 5
St David Rd. CH43: C'ton . . .1E 21
CH62: East 5E 37
St Davids Dr. CH66: Gt Sut . .6A 48
St Davids La. CH43: Noct 2B 20
St Domingo Gro. L5: Liv 5H 7
St Domingo Rd. L5: Liv 4G 7
St Domingo Va. L5: Liv 5H 7
St Edmond's Rd. L20: Boot . . .1E 7
St Edmund's Rd.
CH63: Beb 4F 29
St Edwards Cl. CH41: Birk . . .5F 13
St Elmo Rd. CH44: Wall 6H 5
St Georges Av. CH42: Tran . . .5H 21
CH66: Gt Sut 6A 48
St Georges Ct. CH45: Wall . . .6C 4
St George's Gro.
CH46: More 5D 10
St George's Hgts. L5: Liv 6G 7
St George's Hill L5: Liv 6G 7
St George's Mt.
CH45: New B 3F 5
St George's Pk.
CH45: New B 3F 5
St George's Pl. L1: Liv 3F 15
St George's Rd. CH45: Wall . . .5C 4
St George's Way
CH63: Thorn H 4A 34
L1: Liv 3F 15
(off St Johns Cen.)
St Gerald's Cl. L5: Liv 5F 7
St Helens Cl. CH43: C'ton . . .1F 21
St Hilary Brow
CH44: Wall 1D 12
St Hilary Dr. CH45: Wall 6D 4
St Hilda St. L4: Walt 3G 7
St Hugh's Cl. CH43: C'ton . . .1F 21
St Ives Cl. CH43: C'ton 6E 13
St Ives Rd. CH43: C'ton 1E 21
St James Cl. CH49: Grea 3D 18
St James Cl. CH45: New B . . .3F 5
St James Pl. L8: Liv 6G 15
St James Rd. CH41: Birk 5D 12
CH45: New B 3F 5
L1: Liv 6G 15
St James St. L1: Liv 6F 15
St John's Cen. L1: Liv 4F 15
St John's Ho. L20: Boot 1F 7
St John's La. L1: Liv 3F 15
St John's Pavement
CH41: Birk 1H 21
St John's Rd. CH45: Wall 6C 4
CH62: East 6E 37
L20: Boot 1D 6
L20: Kirk 3E 7

St John's Sq. CH41: Birk 1H 21
L1: Liv 4F 15
(off St Johns Cen.)
St John's Ter. L20: Boot 1D 6
St John St. CH41: Birk 1H 21
St Johns Way L1: Liv 4F 15
St Josephs Cres. L3: Liv 2F 15
St Kilda Cl. CH65: Ell P 6A 50
St Kilda's Rd. CH46: More 6E 11
St Laurence Cl. CH41: Birk . . .6H 13
St Laurence Dr. CH41: Birk . . .6H 13
St Lawrence Cl. L8: Liv 3H 23
St Lucia Rd. CH44: Wall 6H 5
St Luke's Ct. L4: Walt 1H 7
St Lukes Pl. L1: Liv 5G 15
St Margaret's Rd.
CH47: Hoy 1C 16
St Marks Ct. CH43: O'ton 2F 21
St Marks Cres.
CH66: Gt Sut 6A 48
St Martins Dr.
CH66: Gt Sut 5D 48
St Martin's Ho. L20: Boot 1E 7
St Martin's Mkt. L5: Liv 6G 7
St Martins M. L5: Liv 1G 15
St Mary's Av. CH44: Wall 1F 13
L4: Walt 1H 7
St Mary's Ct. CH45: Upton . . .3G 19
St Mary's Ga. CH41: Birk 1B 22
St Mary's Gro. L4: Walt 1H 7
St Mary's La. L4: Walt 1H 7
St Mary's Pl. L4: Walt 1H 7
St Mary's St. CH44: Wall 1F 13
St Michael's Gro.
CH46: More 5D 10
St Michaels Pk.
CH62: Port S 3H 29
St Nicholas Pl. L3: Liv 4D 14
(not continuous)
St Nicholas' Rd. CH45: Wall . . .6B 4
St Oswald's Av. CH43: Bid . . .1A 12
St Oswald's M. CH43: Bid 4A 12
St Paul's Av. CH44: Wall 6H 5
St Paul's Cl. CH42: R Ferr . . .5A 22
St Pauls Gdns.
CH66: Lit Sut 6B 42
St Pauls Pl. L20: Boot 1F 7
St Paul's Rd. CH42: R Ferr . . .5B 22
(not continuous)
CH44: Wall 3H 13
St Paul's Sq. L3: Liv 3D 15
St Paul's Vs. CH42: R Ferr . . .5A 22
St Peters Cl. CH60: Hes 4B 32
St Peter's Ho. L20: Boot 1F 7
St Peter's M. CH42: R Ferr . . .6C 22
St Peter's Rd. CH42: R Ferr . . .6C 22
St Peter's Sq. L1: Liv 5F 15
(off Bk. Colquitt St.)
St Peter's Way
CH43: Noct 3A 20
St Richards Cl. L20: Kirk 2F 7
St Seiriol Gro. CH43: C'ton . . .1E 21
St Stephens Cl. CH60: Hes . . .5E 33
St Stephen's Ct.
CH42: Tran 6F 21
St Stephen's Pl. L3: Liv 2F 15
St Stephen's Rd.
CH42: Tran 6F 21
St Thomas Vw. CH65: Whit . . .3H 49
St Vincent Rd. CH43: C'ton . . .1E 21
CH44: Wall 6H 5
St Vincent St. L3: Liv 3G 15
St Vincent Way L3: Liv 3G 15
St Werburghs Sq.
CH41: Birk 1H 21
St Winifred Rd.
CH45: New B 4F 5
Saker St. L4: Walt 4H 7
Salacre Cl. CH49: Upton 3H 19
Salacre Cres. CH49: Upton . . .3G 19
Salacre La. CH49: Upton 2G 19
Salacre Ter. CH49: Upton 2G 19
Salem Vw. CH43: O'ton 1F 21
Salisbury Av. CH48: W Kir 5C 16
Salisbury Cl. CH66: Gt Sut . . .6A 42
Salisbury Dr. CH62: New F . . .2H 29
Salisbury Rd. CH45: New B . . .3E 5
L5: Liv 5H 7

Salisbury St. CH41: Birk 2H 21
L3: Liv 1G 15
(not continuous)
Salop St. L4: Walt 3H 7
Saltburn Rd. CH45: Wall 6B 4
Saltergate Rd. L8: Liv 3H 23
Saltersgate CH66: Gt Sut 5F 49
Salthouse Quay L3: Liv 5E 15
Saltney St. L3: Liv 6D 6
Samaria Av. CH62: New F 2A 30
Sandalwood Dr.
CH43: Noct 3B 20
Sandbeck St. L8: Liv 4H 23
Sandbourne CH46: More 5G 11
Sandbrook Ct. CH46: More . . .5E 11
Sandbrook La. CH46: More . . .5E 11
Sandcliffe Rd. CH45: Wall 3C 4
Sandfield Av. CH47: Meols . . .4F 9
Sandfield Cl. CH63: High B . . .3D 28
Sandfield Pk. CH60: Hes 3H 31
Sandfield Pk. CH45: New B . . .4F 5
CH49: W'chu 6H 19
CH63: High B 3D 28
L20: Boot 1F 7
Sandfield Ter. CH45: New B . . .4F 5
Sandford St. CH41: Birk 6A 14
Sandham Gro. CH60: Hes 3E 33
Sandhey Rd. CH47: Meols 5E 9
Sandheys CH64: Park 4A 38
Sandheys Cl. L4: Walt 4G 7
Sandhills, The CH46: Leas . . .2E 11
Sandhills Bus. Pk. L5: Kirk . . .4E 7
Sandhills Ind. Est. L5: Kirk . . .5E 7
Sandhills La. L5: Kirk 4D 6
Sandhills Station (Rail) 4E 7
Sandhills Vw. CH45: Wall 6B 4
Sandino St. L8: Liv 1G 23
Sandiway CH47: Meols 4F 9
CH63: Brom 5A 36
Sandiways Rd. CH45: Wall . . .5C 4
Sandlea Pk. CH48: W Kir 5C 16
Sandon Cen. CH64: Lit N 2C 44
Sandon Ind. Est.
L5: Kirk 5D 6
Sandon Prom. CH44: Wall 1H 13
Sandon Rd. CH44: Wall 1H 13
Sandon St. L8: Liv 5H 15
Sandon Way L5: Kirk 5D 6
Sandpiper Cl. CH45: Upton . . .1D 18
Sandpipers Ct. CH47: Hoy 6C 8
Sandridge Rd. CH45: New B . .4F 5
CH61: Pens 4B 26
Sandringham Av.
CH47: Meols 5E 9
Sandringham Cl.
CH47: Meols 5E 9
CH62: New F 2G 29
Sandringham Dr.
CH45: New B 3E 5
Sandringham Gdns.
CH65: Ell P 5B 50
Sandringham M.
CH47: Meols 6E 9
Sandrock Rd. CH45: New B . . .4F 5
Sandstone CH45: Wall 6G 5
Sandstone Dr. CH48: W Kir . . .5G 17
Sandstone Wlk.
CH60: Hes 4C 32
Sandy La. CH45: Wall 5C 4
CH48: W Kir 6D 16
CH60: Hes 2C 32
CH61: Irby 2G 25
CH64: Lit N 6E 39
Sandy La. Nth. CH61: Irby . . .2G 25
Sandymount Dr.
CH45: Wall 4E 5
CH63: Beb 5F 29
Sandy Way CH43: O'ton 2E 21
Sankey St. L1: Liv 5G 15
Sark Av. CH65: Ell P 6H 49
SAUGHALL MASSIE 1C 18
Saughall Massie La.
CH49: Upton 2F 19
Saughall Massie Rd.
CH48: W Kir 4F 17
CH49: Grea, Upton 4F 17
(not continuous)
Saughall Rd. CH46: More 6C 10

Saxon Rd.—Southwick Rd.

Saxon Rd. CH46: More 4F **11**
CH47: Meols 5E **9**
Saxon Way CH66: Gt Sut 6A **48**
Scafell Cl. CH62: East 2F **41**
Scholars Ct. *CH64: Nest 5C 38*
(off Cross St.)
School Av. CH64: Lit N 1D **44**
School Cl. CH46: More 3F **11**
Schoolfield Cl.
CH49: W'chu 5H **19**
Schoolfield Rd.
CH49: W'chu 5H **19**
School Hill CH60: Hes 4B **32**
School La. CH43: Bid 4A **12**
CH44: Wall 6C **4**
CH45: Wall 1C **12**
(not continuous)
CH47: Hoy 6D **8**
(not continuous)
CH47: Meols 4F **9**
CH61: Thurs 3F **25**
CH62: New F 2H **29**
CH63: High B 3D **28**
CH64: Lit N 1D **44**
CH64: Nest 3F **39**
CH64: Park 4A **38**
CH66: Chil T 4H **41**
L1: Liv 4F **15**
School Pl. CH41: Birk 6H **13**
School Rd. CH65: Ell P 2H **49**
Schubert Cl. CH66: Gt Sut 3F **49**
Scilly Cl. CH65: Ell P 6A **50**
Scoresby Rd. CH46: Leas 2A **12**
Scotia Av. CH62: New F 2A **30**
Scotland Rd. L3: Liv 2F **15**
L5: Liv 1F **15**
Scott Cl. L4: Walt 4H **7**
Scotton Av. CH66: Lit Sut 2B **48**
Scotts Pl. CH41: Birk 6D **12**
Scotts Quays CH41: Birk 4A **14**
Scott St. CH45: Wall 6F **5**
Scythes, The CH49: Grea 3C **18**
Scythia Cl. CH62: New F 1A **30**
Seabank Av. CH44: Wall 6G **5**
Seabank Cotts. CH47: Meols 3H **9**
Seabank Rd. CH44: Wall 3F **5**
CH45: New B 3F **5**
CH60: Hes 5A **32**
Sea Brow L1: Liv 4E **15**
Seacombe Dr.
CH66: Gt Sut 4E **49**
Seacombe Prom.
CH44: Wall 1A **14**
(not continuous)
Seacombe Vw. CH44: Wall 3A **14**
Sea Ct. Flats CH45: Wall 4D **4**
Seafield Av. CH60: Hes 5A **32**
Seafield Dr. CH45: Wall 4D **4**
Seafield Rd. CH62: New F 1H **29**
Seaforth Dr. CH46: More 6E **11**
Sealy Cl. CH63: Spit 2G **35**
Sea Rd. CH45: Wall 3D **4**
Seaton Rd. CH42: Tran 3G **21**
CH45: Wall 5E **5**
Sea Vw. CH47: Hoy 6D **8**
CH64: Lit N 3C **44**
Seaview Av. CH45: Wall 6E **5**
CH61: Irby 3H **25**
CH62: East 5F **37**
Seaview La. CH61: Irby 3H **25**
Seaview Rd. CH45: Wall 5E **5**
Seawood Gro. CH46: More 6D **10**
Second Av. CH43: Bid 1H **19**
Sedbergh Rd. CH44: Wall 6D **4**
Seddon St. L1: Liv 5F **15**
Sedgefield Cl. CH46: More 5G **11**
Sedgefield Rd.
CH46: More 5G **11**
Seeley Av. CH41: Birk 6E **13**
Seel St. L1: Liv 4F **15**
Sefton Rd. CH42: R Ferr 6C **22**
CH45: New B 4F **5**
CH62: New F 1G **29**
Sefton St. L8: Liv 1F **23**
Seiont Ho. L8: Liv 2H **23**
Selborne Cl. L8: Liv 6H **15**
Selborne St. L8: Liv 6H **15**
Selbourne Cl. CH49: W'chu 4A **20**
Selby Grn. CH66: Lit Sut 2B **48**
Selby St. CH45: Wall 6F **5**
Selina Rd. L4: Walt 1G **7**
Selkirk Av. CH62: East 1G **41**
Selkirk Cl. CH66: Lit Sut 2H **47**
Sellar St. L4: Kirk 4G **7**
Selston Cl. CH63: Spit 1G **35**
Selwyn St. L4: Kirk 2G **7**
Serpentine Rd. CH44: Wall 6G **5**
Servite Cl. CH65: Ell P 1F **49**
Servite Pl. CH64: Nest 6C **38**
Sessions Rd. L4: Kirk 3F **7**
Seven Acres La.
CH61: Thing 4C **26**
Sevenoaks Cl. L5: Liv 6G **7**
Seven Row CH64: Lit N 2C **44**
Severn St. CH41: Birk 4E **13**
L5: Liv 5H **7**
Severnvale CH65: Whit 4H **49**
Seymour Ct. CH42: Tran 3A **22**
Seymour Dr. CH66: Ell P 1E **49**
Seymour Pl. E. CH45: New B 3F **5**
Seymour Pl. W.
CH45: New B 3F **5**
Seymour St. CH42: Tran 3H **21**
CH45: New B 3F **5**
L3: Liv 3G **15**
L20: Boot 1D **6**
Seymour Ter. *L3: Liv 3G 15*
(off Seymour St.)
Shackleton Rd. CH46: Leas 1H **11**
Shadwell St. L5: Liv 5D **6**
Shaftesbury St. L8: Liv 1G **23**
Shakespeare Av.
CH42: R Ferr 6B **22**
Shakespeare Rd.
CH44: Wall 3H **13**
CH64: Nest 4C **38**
Shalem Ct. CH63: High B 3D **28**
Shalford Gro. CH48: W Kir 5F **17**
Shallmarsh Cl.
CH63: High B 4D **28**
Shallmarsh Ct.
CH63: High B 4D **28**
Shallmarsh Rd.
CH63: High B 4D **28**
Shamrock Rd. CH41: Birk 6D **12**
Shannon Ho. CH46: Leas 1E **11**
Shannon St. CH41: Birk 4D **12**
Sharpeville Cl. L4: Kirk 4F **7**
Shavington Av.
CH43: O'ton 4D **20**
Shawbury Av.
CH63: High B 2D **28**
Shaw Cl. CH66: Gt Sut 3F **49**
Shaw Hill St. L1: Liv 3F **15**
Shaw La. CH49: Grea 5C **18**
Shaws All. L1: Liv 5E **15**
Shaws Dr. CH47: Meols 5F **9**
Shaw St. CH41: Birk 2G **21**
CH47: Hoy 6D **8**
L6: Liv 1H **15**
Shearman Cl. CH61: Pens 5C **26**
Shearman Rd. CH61: Pens 5C **26**
Sheehan Hgts. L5: Liv 5E **7**
Sheen Rd. CH45: New B 5G **5**
Sheepfield Cl.
CH66: Lit Sut 6C **42**
Sheldon Cl. CH63: Spit 2G **35**
Sheldrake Gro. CH64: Lit N 2C **44**
Shelley Way CH48: W Kir 1A **24**
Shellway Rd. CH65: Ell P 4D **50**
Shelmore Dr. L8: Liv 3G **23**
Shelton Rd. CH45: Wall 5E **5**
Shenley Cl. CH63: Beb 3F **29**
Shepherd Cl. CH49: Grea 3C **18**
Shepherd St. L6: Liv 3H **15**
Shepsides Cl.
CH66: Gt Sut 4C **48**
Shepston Av. L4: Walt 2H **7**
Shepton Rd. CH66: Gt Sut 5E **49**
Sherborne Rd. CH44: Wall 6D **4**
Sherbourne Rd.
CH65: Ell P 4B **50**
Sheriff Cl. L5: Liv 1G **15**
Sheringham Cl.
CH49: Upton 6G **11**
Sherlock La. CH44: Wall 3E **13**
Sherry La. CH49: W'chu 5G **19**
Sherwood Av. CH61: Irby 3H **25**
Sherwood Dr.
CH63: High B 2E **29**
Sherwood Gro. CH47: Meols 5H **9**
Sherwood Rd. CH44: Wall 2G **13**
CH47: Meols 6H **9**
Sherwood St. L3: Liv 6D **6**
Shetland Dr. CH62: Brom 3C **36**
CH65: Ell P 6A **50**
Shewell Cl. CH42: Tran 3H **21**
Shiel Rd. CH45: New B 4F **5**
Shipton Cl. CH43: Pren 6C **20**
Shirley St. CH44: Wall 2A **14**
Shones Cft. CH64: Ness 2E **45**
Shore Bank CH62: New F 1A **30**
Shore Dr. CH62: Port S 3A **30**
Shorefields CH62: New F 1H **29**
Shorefields Ho.
CH62: New F 2A **30**
Shorefields Village L8: Liv 4H **23**
Shore La. CH48: Caldy 2A **24**
Shore Rd. CH41: Birk 6A **14**
CH48: Caldy 2A **24**
Shore Road Pumping Station
6B **14**
Shortfield Rd.
CH49: Upton 3G **19**
Shortfield Way
CH49: Upton 3G **19**
Shotwick-Helsby By-Pass
CH1: Back 6A **48**
CH65: Whit 6A **50**
Shrewsbury Cl.
CH43: C'ton 1D **20**
Shrewsbury Dr.
CH49: Upton 1G **19**
Shrewsbury Rd.
CH43: C'ton 6D **12**
CH44: Wall 6D **4**
CH48: W Kir 6C **16**
CH60: Hes 2C **32**
CH65: Ell P 2A **50**
Sidings, The CH42: R Ferr 5B **22**
Sidlaw Cl. CH66: Lit Sut 1A **48**
Sidney Av. CH45: New B 3E **5**
Sidney Cl. CH64: Nest 4D **38**
Sidney Ct. CH42: Tran 3A **22**
Sidney Rd. CH42: Tran 3A **22**
CH64: Nest 4D **38**
L20: Boot 1F **7**
Sidney St. CH41: Birk 6A **14**
Sidney Ter. CH42: Tran 4A **22**
Silkhouse Ct. L3: Liv 3E **15**
Silkhouse La. L2: Liv 3E **15**
Silverbeech Rd.
CH44: Wall 2G **13**
Silver Birches CH66: Whit 6A **48**
Silverbirch Gdns.
CH44: Wall 6C **4**
Silverbirch Way
CH66: Whit 6A **48**
Silverburn Av. CH46: More 4E **11**
Silverdale Rd. CH43: O'ton 3E **21**
CH63: High B 2F **29**
Silverlea Av. CH45: Wall 6E **5**
Silverne Dr. CH65: Whit 5G **49**
Silvester St. L5: Liv 6E **7**
Simon Ct. CH48: W Kir 5C **16**
Simonsbridge CH48: Caldy 3B **24**
Simpson St. CH41: Birk 1H **21**
L1: Liv 6F **15**
Sim St. L3: Liv 2G **15**
Singleton Av. CH42: Tran 4G **21**
Singleton Rd. CH65: Gt Sut 3F **49**
Sir Howard St. L8: Liv 5H **15**
Sir Howard Way L8: Liv 5H **15**
Sir Thomas St. L1: Liv 3E **15**
Sisters Way CH41: Birk 1H **21**
Skelhorne St. L3: Liv 4F **15**
Skiddaw Rd. CH62: Brom 1C **36**
Skipton Dr. CH66: Lit Sut 3C **48**
Skirving St. L5: Liv 5F **7**
Skye Cl. CH65: Ell P 6A **50**
Slater Pl. L1: Liv 5F **15**
Slater St. L1: Liv 5F **15**
Slatey Rd. CH43: O'ton 1F **21**
Sleepers Hill L4: Walt 4H **7**
Slessor Av. CH48: W Kir 4F **17**
Slingsby Dr. CH49: Upton 3G **19**
Smallacres CH65: Ell P 6F **43**
Smallridge Cl. CH61: Pens 5A **26**
Smallwoods M. CH60: Hes 1A **32**
Smeaton St. L4: Kirk 2G **7**
(not continuous)
Smilie Av. CH46: More 4C **10**
Smith Av. CH41: Birk 5F **13**
Smithdown La. L7: Liv 4H **15**
Smithfield St. L3: Liv 3E **15**
Smith Pl. L5: Kirk 5F **7**
Smith St. L5: Kirk 4F **7**
Smithy Cl. CH64: Ness 3E **45**
Smithy Ct. CH66: Lit Sut 1C **48**
Smithy Hey CH48: W Kir 5E **17**
Smithy Hill CH63: Thorn H 5A **34**
Smithy La. CH64: Will 5C **40**
CH66: Lit Sut 1C **48**
L4: Walt 1H **7**
Smugglers Way CH45: Wall 3C **4**
Snab La. CH64: Ness 3D **44**
Snabwood Cl. CH64: Lit N 2C **44**
Snowberry Way
CH66: Whit 6A **48**
Snowden Rd. CH46: More 5C **10**
CH65: Ell P 2A **50**
Snowdon Cl. CH66: Lit Sut 1A **48**
Snowdon La. L5: Liv 6E **7**
Snowdon Rd. CH42: Tran 5H **21**
Snowdrop Av. CH41: Birk 5D **12**
Snowdrop St. L5: Kirk 4F **7**
Soho Pl. L3: Liv 2G **15**
Soho St. L3: Liv 2G **15**
(not continuous)
Solly Av. CH42: R Ferr 5A **22**
Solway St. CH41: Birk 4E **13**
Somerset Rd. CH45: Wall 6C **4**
CH48: W Kir 4E **17**
CH61: Pens 5A **26**
Somerville Cl.
CH63: Brom 5H **35**
CH64: Lit N 2C **44**
Somerville Cres.
CH65: Ell P 3A **50**
Somerville St. Cl. L5: Liv 5G **7**
Sorrel Cl. CH43: Noct 2B **20**
South Bank CH43: O'ton 4F **21**
Southbourne Rd. CH45: Wall 6B **4**
Sth. Chester St. L8: Liv 1G **23**
Southcroft Rd. CH45: Wall 6B **4**
Southdale Rd.
CH42: R Ferr 5A **22**
South Dr. CH49: Upton 2G **19**
CH60: Hes 4C **32**
CH61: Irby 4G **25**
Southern Cres. L8: Liv 2F **23**
Sth. Ferry Quay L3: Liv 1E **23**
Southfield Rd.
CH66: Lit Sut 1C **48**
South Gro. L8: Liv 3H **23**
Sth. Hey Rd. CH61: Irby 5H **25**
Sth. Hill Gro. CH43: O'ton 4F **21**
Sth. Hill Rd. CH43: O'ton 3F **21**
L8: Liv 4H **23**
Sth. Hunter St. L1: Liv 5G **15**
Sth. John St. L1: Liv 4E **15**
(not continuous)
L2: Liv 4E **15**
South Pde. CH48: W Kir 5C **16**
CH64: Park 5A **38**
South Pk. Ct. CH44: Wall 2A **14**
South Pk. Way L20: Boot 1F **7**
Sth. Pier Rd. CH65: Ell P 2H **43**
Southport Rd. L20: Boot 1G **7**
South Quay L3: Liv 5E **15**
Southridge Rd. CH61: Pens 4C **26**
South Rd. CH42: Tran 4G **21**
CH48: W Kir 6D **16**
CH65: Ell P 2D **50**
(Bridges Rd.)
CH65: Ell P 4A **50**
(Malvern Av.)
CH65: Hoot 2C **42**
Sth. Sefton Bus. Cen.
L20: Boot 1D **6**
South St. L8: Liv 2H **23**
South Vw. CH62: Brom 4B **30**
South Vs. CH45: New B 4F **5**
Southwell Pl. L8: Liv 2G **23**
Southwell St. L8: Liv 2G **23**
Southwick Rd. CH42: Tran 4A **22**

Sth. Wirral Retail Pk.—Tarleton St.

Sth. Wirral Retail Pk.
CH62: Brom . . . 6B **30**
Sovereign Way CH44: Wall . . . 4H **13**
Sparks La. CH61: Thing . . . 3D **26**
Sparling St. L1: Liv . . . 6F **15**
(not continuous)
Spear St. L8: Liv . . . 2H **23**
Speedwell Cl. CH60: Hes . . . 3E **33**
Speedwell Dr. CH60: Hes . . . 3E **33**
Speedwell Rd. CH41: Birk . . . 6D **12**
Spellow La. L4: Walt . . . 3H **7**
Spellow Pl. *L3: Liv . . . 3D 14*
(off Union St.)
Spencer Av. CH46: More . . . 4G **11**
Spencer St. L6: Liv . . . 1H **15**
Spenser Av. CH42: R Ferr . . . 6B **22**
Spenser Rd. CH64: Nest . . . 4C **38**
Spindle Cl. L6: Liv . . . 1H **15**
Spindrift Ct. CH48: W Kir . . . 6C **16**
Spinney, The CH48: W Kir . . . 5G **17**
CH49: Upton . . . 1G **19**
CH60: Hes . . . 6E **33**
CH63: Spit . . . 6H **29**
CH64: Park . . . 5A **38**
Spinney Dr. CH66: Gt Sut . . . 4D **48**
SPITAL . . . **6H 29**
Spital Heyes CH63: Spit . . . 6H **29**
Spital Rd.
CH62: Brom, Spit . . . 6A **30**
CH63: Spit . . . 6G **29**
Spital Station (Rail) . . . **6H 29**
Sprainger St. L3: Liv . . . 1D **14**
Spring Av. CH66: Lit Sut . . . 1C **48**
Springcroft CH64: Park . . . 4A **38**
Springdale Rd.
CH46: More . . . 4G **11**
Springfield L3: Liv . . . 2G **15**
(not continuous)
Springfield Av.
CH48: W Kir . . . 5H **17**
Springfield Cl.
CH49: W'chu . . . 5A **20**
Springfield Sq.
L4: Walt . . . 3H **7**
Spring Gdns. CH66: Lit Sut . . . 1C **48**
Springhill Av. CH62: Brom . . . 5B **36**
Spring St. CH42: Tran . . . 4B **22**
Spring Va. CH45: Wall . . . 4C **4**
Springwood Way
CH62: New F . . . 1G **29**
Spruce Cl. CH42: Tran . . . 3H **21**
Spunhill Av. CH66: Gt Sut . . . 5C **48**
Spurgeon Cl. L5: Liv . . . 6H **7**
Spurstow Cl. CH43: O'ton . . . 4D **20**
Squibb Dr. CH46: Leas . . . 3G **11**
Stable Cl. CH49: Grea . . . 3D **18**
Stackfield, The
CH48: W Kir . . . 4H **17**
Stadium Rd. CH62: Brom . . . 6C **30**
Staffin Av. CH65: Ell P . . . 6H **49**
Stafford Gdns.
CH65: Ell P . . . 2H **49**
Staffordshire Cl.
L5: Liv . . . 5G **7**
Stafford St. L3: Liv . . . 3G **15**
Stakes, The CH46: Leas . . . 2E **11**
Stamford St. CH65: Ell P . . . 2G **49**
Stanbury Av. CH63: Beb . . . 3G **29**
Standard Pl. CH42: R Ferr . . . 4B **22**
Standish St. L3: Liv . . . 2F **15**
Stanfield Av. L5: Liv . . . 6H **7**
Stanfield Dr. CH63: Beb . . . 6F **29**
Stanford Av. CH45: New B . . . 4F **5**
Stanhope Dr. CH62: Brom . . . 2B **36**
Stanhope St. L8: Liv . . . 1F **23**
(not continuous)
Stanlaw Abbey Bus. Cen.
CH65: Ell P . . . 5B **50**
Stanlaw Rd. CH65: Ell P . . . 3A **50**
Stanley Av. CH45: Wall . . . 5B **4**
CH63: High B . . . 1B **28**
Stanley Cl. CH44: Wall . . . 3A **14**
L4: Kirk . . . 4F **7**
Stanley Ct. CH42: Tran . . . 4B **22**
Stanley La. CH62: East . . . 1H **41**
Stanley Pct. L20: Boot . . . 1E **7**
Stanley Rd. CH41: Birk . . . 4D **12**
CH47: Hoy . . . 2A **16**
CH62: New F . . . 1G **29**
Stanley Rd. CH65: Ell P . . . 2G **43**
L5: Kirk . . . 1E **7**
L20: Boot, Kirk . . . 1E **7**
Stanley St. CH44: Wall . . . 3A **14**
L1: Liv . . . 3E **15**
Stanley Ter. CH45: New B . . . 4F **5**
L8: Liv . . . 6H 15
(off Up. Parliament St.)
Stanley Theatre *L7: Liv . . . 4H 15*
(off Mt. Pleasant)
Stanmore Pk. CH49: Grea . . . 4B **18**
Stanney Cl. CH62: East . . . 2G **41**
CH64: Nest . . . 6C **38**
Stanney La. CH65: Ell P . . . 3H **49**
(not continuous)
Stanney Mill Ind. Est.
CH2: Lit Stan . . . 4D **50**
Stanney Mill La.
CH2: Lit Stan . . . 6D **50**
Stanney Mill Rd.
CH2: Lit Stan . . . 4D **50**
Stanney Oaks Leisure Cen.
. . . **5B 50**
Stanney Ten Ind. Est.
CH2: Lit Stan . . . 5D **50**
Stanney Woods Av.
CH65: Ell P . . . 6A **50**
Stanton Cl. CH64: Nest . . . 5C **38**
Stanton Ct. *CH64: Nest . . . 5C 38*
(off Hinderton Rd.)
Stanton Rd. CH63: Beb . . . 6E **29**
Stapleford Ct. CH66: Ell P . . . 5F **43**
Stapleton Av. CH49: Grea . . . 3D **18**
Starbeck Dr. CH66: Lit Sut . . . 1B **48**
Star St. L8: Liv . . . 1G **23**
Starworth Dr. CH62: New F . . . 2A **30**
Statham Rd. CH43: Bid . . . 5A **12**
Station App. CH46: More . . . 3E **11**
CH47: Meols . . . 5G **9**
Station Av. CH66: Lit Sut . . . 6C **42**
Station Cl. CH64: Nest . . . 6D **38**
Station Grn. CH66: Lit Sut . . . 6C **42**
Station Rd. CH41: Birk . . . 4D **12**
CH44: Wall . . . 1E **13**
CH47: Hoy . . . 1D **16**
CH60: Hes . . . 5B **32**
CH61: Barn . . . 4F **27**
CH61: Thurs . . . 6D **24**
CH63: Store . . . 4F **27**
CH64: Burt . . . 5E **45**
CH64: Nest . . . 6C **38**
(not continuous)
CH64: Park . . . 5A **38**
CH65: Ell P . . . 1A **50**
(not continuous)
CH66: Lit Sut . . . 1C **48**
Stavordale Rd.
CH46: More . . . 4G **11**
Steble St. L8: Liv . . . 2H **23**
Steel Av. CH45: Wall . . . 5G **5**
Steel Ct. L5: Liv . . . 5E **7**
Steeple, The CH48: Caldy . . . 3B **24**
Steeple Ct. CH64: Nest . . . 6C **38**
Steinberg Ct. L3: Liv . . . 1E **15**
Stephens Gdns.
CH66: Lit Sut . . . 1B **48**
Stephens La. L2: Liv . . . 3E **15**
Stephens Ter.
CH66: Lit Sut . . . 1B **48**
Stepney Gro. L4: Walt . . . 2H **7**
Sterling Way L5: Kirk . . . 5F **7**
Stevenson Dr. CH63: Spit . . . 6F **29**
Stevens Rd. CH60: Hes . . . 4E **33**
Stewart Cl. CH61: Pens . . . 6B **26**
Stillington Rd. L8: Liv . . . 3H **23**
Stiperstones Cl.
CH66: Lit Sut . . . 1H **47**
Stirling Ct. CH65: Ell P . . . 4B **50**
Stirling St. CH44: Wall . . . 3F **13**
Stoak Lodge CH65: Ell P . . . 3A **50**
Stockbridge Pl. L5: Liv . . . 5H **7**
Stockbridge St. L5: Liv . . . 6H **7**
Stockdale Cl. L3: Liv . . . 2E **15**
Stoddart Rd. L4: Walt . . . 1H **7**
Stoke Cl. CH62: East . . . 2G **41**
Stoke Gdns. CH65: Ell P . . . 3A **50**
Stokesay CH43: Noct . . . 1B **20**
Stokesay Ct. CH65: Ell P . . . 4C **50**
Stoke St. CH41: Birk . . . 5F **13**
Stoke Wlk. CH65: Ell P . . . 3A **50**
Stonebank Dr. CH64: Lit N . . . 1E **45**
Stoneby Dr. CH45: Wall . . . 4E **5**
Stonegate Dr. L8: Liv . . . 3H **23**
Stonehey Dr. CH48: W Kir . . . 1A **24**
Stonehill Av. CH63: Beb . . . 3G **29**
Stonehouse Rd.
CH44: Wall . . . 6C **4**
Stoneleigh Gro.
CH42: R Ferr . . . 1F **29**
Stoneridge Ct. CH43: Bid . . . 5A **12**
Stone St. L3: Liv . . . 1D **14**
Stoney Hey Rd.
CH45: New B . . . 4E **5**
Stonham Cl. CH49: Upton . . . 2E **19**
Stopford St. L8: Liv . . . 3H **23**
Store St. L20: Kirk . . . 2F **7**
STORETON . . . **4A 28**
STORETON BRICKFIELDS . . . **4G 27**
Storeton Cl. CH43: O'ton . . . 4E **21**
Storeton La. CH61: Barn . . . 6E **27**
Storeton Rd. CH42: Tran . . . 4F **21**
CH43: O'ton . . . 4F **21**
Stourcliffe Rd. CH44: Wall . . . 1E **13**
Stour Ct. CH65: Ell P . . . 6H **43**
Stourport Cl. CH49: Grea . . . 3C **18**
Stourton St. CH44: Wall . . . 3G **13**
Stowell St. L7: Liv . . . 5H **15**
Strada Way L3: Liv . . . 2H **15**
Straker Av. CH65: Ell P . . . 1F **49**
Strand, The L2: Liv . . . 4D **14**
Strand Rd. CH47: Hoy . . . 6D **8**
Strand St. L1: Liv . . . 4E **15**
Stratford Rd. CH64: Nest . . . 1C **44**
Strathallan Cl. CH60: Hes . . . 1A **32**
Strathcona Rd. CH45: Wall . . . 5F **5**
Strathearn Rd. CH60: Hes . . . 5B **32**
Strathlorne Cl. CH42: Tran . . . 4B **22**
Stratton Cl. CH45: Wall . . . 5G **5**
Strawberry Dr. CH66: Whit . . . 6B **48**
Strawberry Grn.
CH66: Whit . . . 6B **48**
Street Hey La. CH64: Will . . . 2D **40**
Stretton Av. CH44: Wall . . . 1E **13**
Stretton Cl. CH43: O'ton . . . 4C **20**
CH62: East . . . 2G **41**
Stringhey Rd. CH44: Wall . . . 6G **5**
Stroma Av. CH65: Ell P . . . 6H **49**
Stroud Cl. CH49: Grea . . . 4C **18**
Stuart Av. CH46: More . . . 4F **11**
Stuart Cl. CH46: More . . . 5G **11**
Stuart Gro. L20: Kirk . . . 2F **7**
Stuart Rd. CH42: Tran . . . 4H **21**
L4: Walt . . . 1G **7**
Stuart Rd. Nth. L20: Boot . . . 1G **7**
Stubbs La. CH43: Noct . . . 4C **20**
Studholme St. L20: Kirk . . . 4E **7**
Studley Rd. CH45: Wall . . . 5C **4**
Sudworth Rd. CH45: New B . . . 4E **5**
Suffield Rd. L4: Kirk . . . 3F **7**
Suffolk Av. CH65: Ell P . . . 2G **49**
Suffolk St. L1: Liv . . . 5F **15**
Sugnall St. L7: Liv . . . 5H **15**
(not continuous)
Sullivan Av. CH49: Upton . . . 3F **19**
Summerfield CH62: Brom . . . 1B **36**
Summerford Cl.
CH42: Tran . . . 4A **22**
Summer Seat L3: Liv . . . 1E **15**
Summers Rd. L3: Liv . . . 2F **23**
Summertrees Av.
CH49: Grea . . . 3D **18**
Summertrees Cl.
CH49: Grea . . . 3D **18**
Summertrees Rd.
CH66: Gt Sut . . . 5E **49**
Summerwood
CH61: Irby . . . 2H **25**
Summit, The CH44: Wall . . . 6G **5**
Sumner Cl. L5: Liv . . . 6E **7**
Sumner Rd. CH43: Bid . . . 5D **12**
Sunbury Rd. CH44: Wall . . . 2G **13**
Suncroft Rd. CH60: Hes . . . 4E **33**
Sundridge St. L8: Liv . . . 3H **23**
Sunfield Cl. CH66: Gt Sut . . . 4D **48**
Sunfield Rd. CH46: More . . . 3F **11**
Sunlight Lodge
CH62: Port S . . . 3H **29**
Sunningdale CH46: More . . . 5G **11**
Sunningdale Dr.
CH61: Thing . . . 4C **26**
CH63: Brom . . . 5H **35**
Sunningdale Rd. CH45: Wall . . . 3D **4**
Sunningdale Way
CH64: Lit N . . . 2C **44**
Sunny Bank CH63: High B . . . 3D **28**
Sunnybank CH49: Upton . . . 1F **19**
Sunnybank Av. CH43: Noct . . . 3B **20**
Sunnyside CH46: More . . . 3D **10**
CH65: Ell P . . . 1A 50
(off Church St.)
Surrey Av. CH49: Upton . . . 2F **19**
Surrey Dr. CH48: W Kir . . . 1A **24**
Surrey St. CH44: Wall . . . 2E **13**
L1: Liv . . . 5F **15**
Susan Gro. CH46: More . . . 5D **10**
Sussex Cl. CH61: Pens . . . 5A **26**
Sussex Rd. CH48: W Kir . . . 4E **17**
Sutherland Dr. CH62: East . . . 1F **41**
Sutton Av. CH64: Nest . . . 1C **44**
Sutton Cl. CH62: East . . . 2G **41**
SUTTON GREEN . . . **4C 48**
Sutton Hall Dr.
CH66: Lit Sut . . . 1A **48**
Sutton Hall Gdns.
CH66: Lit Sut . . . 1A **48**
Sutton Rd. CH45: New B . . . 4F **5**
Sutton Sports Cen. . . . **1E 49**
Sutton Way
CH65: Gt Sut, Whit . . . 2F **49**
CH66: Gt Sut . . . 3D **48**
Swaledale Cl. CH62: East . . . 6C **36**
Swale Rd. CH65: Ell P . . . 6G **43**
Swan Cl. CH66: Gt Sut . . . 5D **48**
Swan Ct. CH43: Pren . . . 5D **20**
Swanston Av. L4: Walt . . . 2H **7**
Sweetfield Gdns.
CH66: Lit Sut . . . 6D **42**
Sweetfield Rd.
CH66: Lit Sut . . . 6D **42**
Sweeting St. L2: Liv . . . 4E **15**
Swift Weint CH64: Park . . . 4A **38**
Swindon Cl. CH49: Grea . . . 3C **18**
L5: Kirk . . . 4F **7**
Swindon St. L5: Kirk . . . 4F **7**
Sybil Rd. L4: Walt . . . 4H **7**
Sycamore Av. CH49: Upton . . . 6D **10**
Sycamore Cl. CH49: Upton . . . 6D **10**
Sycamore Ct. *L8: Liv . . . 3H 23*
(off Weller Way)
Sycamore Dr. CH66: Whit . . . 6F **49**
Sycamore Ri. CH49: Grea . . . 5C **18**
Sycamore Rd. CH42: Tran . . . 3H **21**
Sylvandale Gro.
CH62: Brom . . . 6B **30**
Syren St. L20: Kirk . . . 3E **7**
Sytch Cft. CH64: Nest . . . 5C **38**

T

Tabley Cl. CH43: O'ton . . . 5D **20**
Tabley St. L1: Liv . . . 5E **15**
Tace Cl. L8: Liv . . . 6H **15**
Talbot Av. CH63: Brim . . . 2A **34**
CH64: Lit N . . . 1D **44**
Talbot Cl. CH64: Lit N . . . 1D **44**
Talbot Ct. CH43: O'ton . . . 3E **21**
Talbot Gdns. CH64: Lit N . . . 1D **44**
Talbot Rd. CH43: O'ton . . . 3E **21**
CH66: Gt Sut . . . 4F **49**
Taliesin St. L5: Liv . . . 6F **7**
Tamar Cl. L6: Liv . . . 1H **15**
Tamar Gro. CH46: More . . . 5D **10**
Tam O'Shanter Urban Farm
. . . **6C 12**
Tamworth St. L8: Liv . . . 2G **23**
Tanar Cl. CH63: Spit . . . 6H **29**
Tancred Rd. CH45: Wall . . . 6E **5**
L4: Walt . . . 4H **7**
Tannery La. CH64: Nest . . . 5C **38**
Tansley Cl. CH48: W Kir . . . 5G **17**
Tanworth Gro. CH46: More . . . 4B **10**
Tara Pk. Cvn. Site L3: Liv . . . 1D **14**
Tarbot Hey CH46: More . . . 5C **10**
Target Rd. CH60: Hes . . . 3G **31**
Tariff St. L5: Liv . . . 6E **7**
Tarleton St. L1: Liv . . . 4F **15**

76 A-Z Wirral

The representation on the maps of a road, track or footpath is no evidence of the existence of a right of way.

The Grid on this map is the National Grid taken from Ordnance Survey mapping with the permission of the Controller of Her Majesty's Stationery Office.